LOW-CHOLESTEROL
COOKBOOK

LOW-CHOLESTEROL
COOKBOOK

130 BEST-EVER LOW-FAT, NO-FAT RECIPES FOR A HEALTHY LIFE

CHRISTINE FRANCE

southwater

This edition is published by Southwater, an imprint of Anness Publishing Ltd, Hermes House, 88–89 Blackfriars Road, London SE1 8HA; tel. 020 7401 2077; fax 020 7633 9499

www.southwaterbooks.com; www.annesspublishing.com

If you like the images in this book and would like to investigate using them for publishing, promotions or advertising, please visit our website www.practicalpictures.com for more information.

UK agent: The Manning Partnership Ltd;
tel. 01225 478444; fax 01225 478440; sales@manning-partnership.co.uk
UK distributor: Grantham Book Services Ltd;
tel. 01476 541080; fax 01476 541061; orders@gbs.tbs-ltd.co.uk
North American agent/distributor: National Book Network;
tel. 301 459 3366; fax 301 429 5746; www.nbnbooks.com
Australian agent/distributor: Pan Macmillan Australia;
tel. 1300 135 113; fax 1300 135 103; customer.service@macmillan.com.au
New Zealand agent/distributor: David Bateman Ltd;
tel. (09) 415 7664; fax (09) 415 8892

Publisher: Joanna Lorenz
Series Editor: Linda Fraser
Copy Editor: Penny David
Designers: Tony Paine and Roy Prescott
Photographer: Karl Adamson
Food for Photography: Jane Stevenson
Props Stylist: Kirsty Rawlings

ETHICAL TRADING POLICY

Because of our ongoing ecological investment programme, you, as our customer, can have the pleasure and reassurance of knowing that a tree is being cultivated on your behalf to naturally replace the materials used to make the book you are holding. For further information about this scheme, go to www.annesspublishing.com/trees

A CIP catalogue record for this book is available from the British Library.

Previously published as *Low Fat, Low Cholesterol*

NOTES

For all recipes, quantities are given in both metric and imperial measures and, where appropriate, in standard cups and spoons.
Follow one set of measures, but not a mixture, because they are not interchangeable.
Standard spoon and cup measures are level. 1 tsp = 5ml, 1 tbsp = 15ml, 1 cup = 250ml/8fl oz.
Australian standard tablespoons are 20ml. Australian readers should use 3 tsp in place of 1 tbsp for measuring small quantities of gelatine, flour, salt, etc.
American pints are 16fl oz/2 cups. American readers should use 20fl oz/2.5 cups in place of 1 pint when measuring liquids.
Electric oven temperatures in this book are for conventional ovens. When using a fan oven, the temperature will probably need to be reduced by about 10–20°C/20–40°F. Since ovens vary, you should check with your manufacturer's instruction book for guidance.
The nutritional analysis given for each recipe is calculated per portion (i.e. serving or item), unless otherwise stated. If the recipe gives a range, such as Serves 4–6, then the nutritional analysis will be for the smaller portion size, i.e. 6 servings. Measurements for sodium do not include salt added to taste.
Medium (US large) eggs are used unless otherwise stated.

Main front cover image shows Middle-Eastern Vegetable Stew - for recipe, see page 102

PUBLISHER'S NOTE

Although the advice and information in this book are believed to be accurate and true at the time of going to press, neither the authors nor the publisher can accept any legal responsibility or liability for any errors or omissions that may be made.

CONTENTS

WHY A LOW FAT DIET?

We need a certain amount of fat in our diet for general health and it is a valuable source of energy. Also, it plays a vital role in making foods palatable to eat. However, most of us eat more fat than we need. You should not try to cut out fat altogether, but a lower fat diet has the benefits of weight loss and reduction in the risk of heart disease.

There are two types of fat – saturated and unsaturated. The unsaturated group includes two types – polyunsaturated and monounsaturated fats.

Saturated fats are the ones you should limit, as they increase cholesterol in the blood, and this can increase the risk of heart disease. The main sources of saturated fat are animal products such as dairy products and meat, but also hard fats and hydrogenated vegetable fat or oil. Polyunsaturated fats are essential in small quantities for good health, and are thought to help reduce the cholesterol in the blood. There is also some evidence that monounsaturated fats have a beneficial effect. The main sources of polyunsaturates are vegetable oils such as sunflower, corn and soya, and oily fish such as herring, mackerel, pilchards, sardines and trout. Sources of monounsaturated fats include olive, rapeseed and groundnut oils, as well as avocadoes and many nuts.

Cutting Down on Cholesterol?

Cholesterol is a substance which occurs naturally in the blood, and is essential for the formation of hormones, body cells, nerves and bile salts which help digestion.

A high cholesterol level can increase the likelihood of coronary heart disease, as it becomes deposited on the walls of the arteries, causing them to fur up. The main cause of raised cholesterol levels is eating too much fat, especially saturated fat. Eating too much saturated fat encourages the body to make more cholesterol than it needs, and also seems to prevent it getting rid of the excess.

The cholesterol found in foods such as egg yolk, offal, cheese, butter and shellfish does not have a major effect on the amount of blood cholesterol in most people, but it is best not to eat large quantities of these foods too often.

Fresh approach: when you are shopping for low fat foods, choose fresh seasonal vegetables (top right) and cook them without added fat. Salads (right) are a good accompaniment too, just use a polyunsaturated or monounsaturated oil for the dressing. Fresh fruits (above) are the perfect ending to a low fat meal if you haven't time to cook – eat them either raw in a salad or poach in fruit juice and serve hot with yogurt.

EASY WAYS TO CUT DOWN FAT AND SATURATED FAT

EAT LESS	TRY INSTEAD
Butter and hard fats.	Try spreading butter more thinly, or replace it with a low fat spread or polyunsaturated margarine.
Fatty meats and high fat products such as pies and sausages.	Buy the leanest cuts of meat you can afford and choose low fat meats like skinless chicken or turkey. Look for reduced-fat sausages and meat products. Eat fish more often, especially oily fish.
Full fat dairy products like cream, butter, hard margarine, milk and hard cheeses.	Choose skimmed or semi-skimmed milk and milk products, and try low fat yogurt, low fat fromage frais and lower fat cheeses such as skimmed milk soft cheese, reduced fat Cheddar, mozzarella or Brie.
Hard cooking fats such as lard or hard margarine.	Choose polyunsaturated oils for cooking, such as olive, sunflower, corn or soya oil.
Rich salad dressings like mayonnaise or salad cream.	Make salad dressings with low fat yogurt or fromage frais, or use a healthy oil such as olive oil.
Fried foods.	Grill, microwave, steam or bake when possible. Roast meats on a rack. Fill up on starchy foods like pasta, rice and couscous. Choose jacket or boiled potatoes, not chips.
Added fat in cooking.	Use heavy-based or non-stick pans so you can cook with little or no added fat.
High fat snacks such as crisps, chocolate, cakes, pastries and biscuits.	Choose fresh or dried fruit, breadsticks or vegetable sticks. Make your own low fat cakes and bakes.

STARTERS AND SNACKS

For a healthy diet it makes good sense to include some home-made soups in everyday meals, packed with the goodness of fresh ingredients and very low in fat. As a light lunch with crusty bread, or as a starter, modern soups are extremely quick and easy to make. The Thai-style Sweetcorn Soup takes only two to three minutes. An added bonus is the variety of fresh, seasonal vegetables available all year. Other starters can double up as a light dish or snack. It pays to have a selection of these healthy, quick snack foods handy. For simple snacks or packed lunches, pittas, Granary rolls or tacos can contain a tasty, low fat filling like chilli-spiced tuna salad. Some snacks are elegant enough for dinner party starters too.

SPLIT PEA AND COURGETTE SOUP

Rich and satisfying, this tasty and nutritious soup will warm a chilly winter's day.

INGREDIENTS

Serves 4

175g/6oz/1⅞ cups yellow split peas
1 medium onion, finely chopped
5ml/1 tsp sunflower oil
2 medium courgettes, finely diced
900ml/1½ pints/3¾ cups chicken stock
2.5ml/½ tsp ground turmeric
salt and black pepper

1 Place the split peas in a bowl, cover with cold water, and leave to soak for several hours or overnight. Drain, rinse in cold water, and drain again.

2 Cook the onion in the oil in a covered pan, shaking occasionally, until soft. Reserve a handful of diced courgette and add the rest to the pan. Cook, stirring, for 2–3 minutes.

3 Add the split peas, stock and turmeric, and bring to the boil. Reduce the heat, cover and simmer for 30–40 minutes, or until the split peas are tender. Adjust the seasoning.

4 When the soup is almost ready, bring a large saucepan of water to the boil, add the reserved diced courgettes, and cook for 1 minute. Drain and add to the soup before serving hot with warm crusty bread.

COOK'S TIP

For a quicker alternative, use split red lentils for this soup – they need no presoaking and cook very quickly. Adjust the amount of stock, if necessary.

NUTRITION NOTES

Per portion:

Energy	174Kcals/730kJ
Fat	2.14g
Saturated fat	0.54g
Cholesterol	0
Fibre	3.43g

RED PEPPER SOUP WITH LIME

The beautiful rich red colour of this soup makes it a very attractive starter or light lunch. For a special dinner, toast some tiny croutons and serve sprinkled into the soup.

INGREDIENTS

Serves 4–6
4 red peppers, seeded and chopped
1 large onion, chopped
5ml/1 tsp olive oil
1 garlic clove, crushed
1 small red chilli, sliced
45ml/3 tbsp tomato purée
900ml/1½ pints/3¾ cups chicken stock
finely grated rind and juice of 1 lime
salt and black pepper
shreds of lime rind, to garnish

1 Cook the onion and peppers gently in the oil in a covered saucepan for about 5 minutes, shaking the pan occasionally, until softened.

2 Stir in the garlic, then add the chilli with the tomato purée. Stir in half the stock, then bring to the boil. Cover the pan and simmer for 10 minutes.

3 Cool slightly, then purée in a food processor or blender. Return to the pan, then add the remaining stock, the lime rind and juice, and seasoning.

4 Bring the soup back to the boil, then serve at once with a few strips of lime rind, scattered into each bowl.

NUTRITION NOTES	
Per portion:	
Energy	87Kcals/366kJ
Fat	1.57g
Saturated fat	0.12g
Cholesterol	0
Fibre	3.40g

CAULIFLOWER AND WALNUT CREAM

Even though there's no cream added to this soup, the cauliflower gives it a delicious, rich, creamy texture.

INGREDIENTS

Serves 4
1 medium cauliflower
1 medium onion, roughly chopped
450ml/¾ pint/1⅞ cups chicken or
    vegetable stock
450ml/¾ pint/1⅞ cups skimmed milk
45ml/3 tbsp walnut pieces
salt and black pepper
paprika and chopped walnuts, to
    garnish

2 Bring to the boil, cover and simmer for about 15 minutes, or until soft. Add the milk and walnuts, then purée in a food processor until smooth.

1 Trim the cauliflower of outer leaves and break into small florets. Place the cauliflower, onion and stock in a large saucepan.

3 Season the soup to taste, then bring to the boil. Serve sprinkled with paprika and chopped walnuts.

NUTRITION NOTES

Per portion:

Energy	166Kcals/699kJ
Fat	9.02g
Saturated fat	0.88g
Cholesterol	2.25mg
Fibre	2.73g

CURRIED CARROT AND APPLE SOUP

INGREDIENTS

Serves 4
10ml/2 tsp sunflower oil
15ml/1 tbsp mild Korma curry powder
500g/1¼ lb carrots, chopped
1 large onion, chopped
1 Bramley cooking apple, chopped
750ml/1¼ pints/3⅔ cups chicken stock
salt and black pepper
natural low fat yogurt and carrot curls,
    to garnish

NUTRITION NOTES

Per portion:

Energy	114Kcals/477kJ
Fat	3.57g
Saturated fat	0.43g
Cholesterol	0.4mg
Fibre	4.99g

1 Heat the oil and gently fry the curry powder for 2–3 minutes.

2 Add the carrots, onion and apple, stir well, then cover the pan.

3 Cook over a very low heat for about 15 minutes, shaking the pan occasionally until softened. Spoon the vegetable mixture into a food processor or blender, then add half the stock and process until smooth.

4 Return to the pan and pour in the remaining stock. Bring the soup to the boil and adjust the seasoning before serving in bowls, garnished with a swirl of yogurt and a few curls of carrot.

MEDITERRANEAN TOMATO SOUP

Children will love this soup –
especially if you use fancy shapes
of pasta such as alphabet or
animal shapes.

INGREDIENTS

Serves 4

675g/1½ lb ripe plum tomatoes
1 medium onion, quartered
1 celery stick
1 garlic clove
15ml/1 tbsp olive oil
450ml/¾ pint/1⅞ cups chicken stock
15ml/2 tbsp tomato purée
50g/2oz/½ cup small pasta shapes
salt and black pepper
fresh coriander or parsley, to garnish

1 Place the tomatoes, onion, celery
and garlic in a pan with the oil.
Cover and cook over a low heat for
40–45 minutes, shaking the pan
occasionally, until very soft.

2 Spoon the vegetables into a food
processor or blender and process
until smooth. Press though a sieve, then
return to the pan.

3 Stir in the stock and tomato purée
and bring to the boil. Add the pasta
and simmer gently for about 8 minutes,
or until the pasta is tender. Add salt
and pepper, to taste, then sprinkle with
coriander or parsley and serve hot.

NUTRITION NOTES

Per portion:

Energy	112Kcals/474kJ
Fat	3.61g
Saturated fat	0.49g
Cholesterol	0
Fibre	2.68g

MUSHROOM, CELERY AND GARLIC SOUP

INGREDIENTS

Serves 4

350g/12oz/3 cups chopped mushrooms
4 celery sticks, chopped
3 garlic cloves
45ml/3 tbsp dry sherry or white wine
750ml/1¼ pints/3⅔cups chicken stock
30ml/2 tbsp Worcestershire sauce
5ml/1 tsp grated nutmeg
salt and black pepper
celery leaves, to garnish

NUTRITION NOTES

Per portion:

Energy	48Kcals/200kJ
Fat	1.09g
Saturated fat	0.11g
Cholesterol	0
Fibre	1.64g

1 Place the mushrooms, celery and
garlic in a pan and stir in the sherry
or wine. Cover and cook over a low
heat for 30–40 minutes, until tender.

2 Add half the stock and purée in a
food processor or blender until
smooth. Return to the pan and add the
remaining stock, the Worcestershire
sauce and nutmeg.

3 Bring to the boil, season and serve
hot, garnished with celery leaves.

BEETROOT AND APRICOT SWIRL

This soup is most attractive if you swirl together the two coloured mixtures, but if you prefer they can be mixed together to save on time and washing up.

INGREDIENTS

Serves 4

4 large cooked beetroot, roughly
    chopped
1 small onion, roughly chopped
600ml/1 pint/2½ cups chicken stock
200g/7oz/1 cup ready-to-eat dried
    apricots
250ml/8 fl oz/1 cup orange juice
salt and black pepper

1 Place the beetroot and half the onion in a pan with the stock. Bring to the boil, then reduce the heat, cover and simmer for about 10 minutes. Purée in a food processor or blender.

2 Place the rest of the onion in a pan with the apricots and orange juice, cover and simmer gently for about 15 minutes, until tender. Purée in a food processor or blender.

3 Return the two mixtures to the saucepans and reheat. Season to taste with salt and pepper, then swirl them together in individual soup bowls for a marbled effect.

COOK'S TIP
The apricot mixture should be the same consistency as the beetroot mixture – if it is too thick, then add a little more orange juice.

NUTRITION NOTES

Per portion:
Energy	135Kcals/569kJ
Fat	0.51g
Saturated fat	0.01g
Cholesterol	0
Fibre	4.43g

THAI-STYLE SWEETCORN SOUP

This is a very quick and easy soup, made in minutes. If you are using frozen prawns, then defrost them first before adding to the soup.

INGREDIENTS

Serves 4

2.5ml/½ tsp sesame or sunflower oil
2 spring onions, thinly sliced
1 garlic clove, crushed
600ml/1 pint/2½ cups chicken stock
425g/15oz can cream-style sweetcorn
225g/8oz/1¼ cups cooked, peeled prawns
5ml/1 tsp green chilli paste or chilli sauce (optional)
salt and black pepper
fresh coriander leaves, to garnish

1 Heat the oil in a large heavy-based saucepan and sauté the onions and garlic over a medium heat for 1 minute, until softened, but not browned.

2 Stir in the chicken stock, cream-style sweetcorn, prawns and chilli paste or sauce, if using.

3 Bring the soup to the boil, stirring occasionally. Season to taste, then serve at once, sprinkled with fresh coriander leaves to garnish.

COOK'S TIP
If cream-style corn is not available, use ordinary canned sweetcorn, puréed in a food processor for a few seconds, until creamy yet with some texture left.

NUTRITION NOTES

Per portion:

Energy	202Kcals/848kJ
Fat	3.01g
Saturated fat	0.43g
Cholesterol	45.56mg
Fibre	1.6g

MUSHROOM CROUSTADES

The rich mushroom flavour of this filling is heightened by the addition of Worcestershire sauce.

INGREDIENTS

Serves 2–4
1 short French stick, about 25cm/10in
10ml/2 tsp olive oil
250g/9oz open cup mushrooms,
  quartered
10ml/2 tsp Worcestershire sauce
10ml/2 tsp lemon juice
30ml/2 tbsp skimmed milk
30ml/2 tbsp snipped fresh chives
salt and black pepper
snipped fresh chives, to garnish

1 Preheat the oven to 200°C/400°F/ Gas 6. Cut the French bread in half lengthways. Cut a scoop out of the soft middle of each, leaving a thick border all the way round.

2 Brush the bread with oil, place on a baking sheet and bake for about 6–8 minutes, until golden and crisp.

3 Place the mushrooms in a small saucepan with the Worcestershire sauce, lemon juice and milk. Simmer for about 5 minutes, or until most of the liquid is evaporated.

4 Remove from the heat, then add the chives and seasoning. Spoon into the bread croustades and serve hot, garnished with snipped chives.

NUTRITION NOTES

Per portion:	
Energy	324Kcals/1361kJ
Fat	6.4g
Saturated fat	1.27g
Cholesterol	0.3mg
Fibre	3.07g

TOMATO PESTO TOASTIES

Ready-made pesto is high in fat but, as its flavour is so powerful, it can be used in very small amounts with good effect, as in these tasty toasties.

INGREDIENTS

Serves 2
2 thick slices crusty bread
45ml/3 tbsp skimmed milk soft cheese or low fat fromage frais
10ml/2 tsp red or green pesto
1 beef tomato
1 red onion
salt and black pepper

1 Toast the bread slices on a hot grill until golden brown on both sides turning once. Leave to cool.

2 Mix together the skimmed milk soft cheese and pesto in a small bowl until well blended, then spread thickly on to the toasted bread.

3 Cut the beef tomato and red onion, crossways, into thin slices using a large sharp knife.

4 Arrange the slices, overlapping, on top of the toast and season with salt and pepper. Transfer the toasties to a grill rack and cook under a hot grill until heated through, then serve immediately.

COOK'S TIP
Almost any type of crusty bread can be used for this recipe, but Italian olive oil bread and French bread will give the best flavour.

NUTRITION NOTES

Per portion:	
Energy	177Kcals/741kJ
Fat	2.41g
Saturated fat	0.19g
Cholesterol	0.23mg
Fibre	2.2g

CHEESE AND SPINACH PUFFS

INGREDIENTS

Serves 6
150g/5oz cooked, chopped spinach
175g/6oz/¾ cup cottage cheese
5ml/1 tsp grated nutmeg
2 egg whites
30ml/2 tbsp grated Parmesan cheese
salt and black pepper

1 Preheat the oven to 220°C/425°F/ Gas 7. Oil six ramekin dishes.

2 Mix together the spinach and cottage cheese in a small bowl, then add the nutmeg and seasoning to taste.

3 Whisk the egg whites in a separate bowl until stiff enough to hold soft peaks. Fold them evenly into the spinach mixture using a spatula or large metal spoon, then spoon the mixture into the oiled ramekins, dividing it evenly, and smooth the tops.

4 Sprinkle with the Parmesan and place on a baking sheet. Bake for 15–20 minutes, or until well risen and golden brown. Serve immediately.

NUTRITION NOTES

Per portion:

Energy	47Kcals/195kJ
Fat	1.32g
Saturated fat	0.52g
Cholesterol	2.79mg
Fibre	0.53g

LEMONY STUFFED COURGETTES

INGREDIENTS

Serves 4
4 courgettes, about 175g/6oz each
5ml/1 tsp sunflower oil
1 garlic clove, crushed
5ml/1 tsp ground lemon grass
finely grated rind and juice of ½ lemon
115g/4oz/1½ cups cooked long grain rice
175g/6oz cherry tomatoes, halved
30ml/2 tbsp toasted cashew nuts
salt and black pepper
sprigs of thyme, to garnish

NUTRITION NOTES

Per portion:

Energy	126Kcals/530kJ
Fat	5.33g
Saturated fat	0.65g
Cholesterol	0
Fibre	2.31g

1 Preheat the oven to 200°C/400°F/ Gas 6. Halve the courgettes lengthways and use a teaspoon to scoop out the centres. Blanch the shells in boiling water for 1 minute, then drain well.

2 Chop the courgette flesh finely and place in a saucepan with the oil and garlic. Stir over a moderate heat until softened, but not browned.

3 Stir in the lemon grass, lemon rind and juice, rice, tomatoes and cashew nuts. Season well and spoon into the courgette shells. Place the shells in a baking tin and cover with foil.

4 Bake for 25–30 minutes or until the courgettes are tender, then serve hot, garnished with thyme sprigs.

CHICKEN PITTAS WITH RED COLESLAW

Pittas are convenient for simple snacks and packed lunches and it's easy to pack in lots of fresh healthy ingredients.

INGREDIENTS

Serves 4

¼ red cabbage, finely shredded
1 small red onion, finely sliced
2 radishes, thinly sliced
1 red apple, peeled, cored and grated
15ml/1 tbsp lemon juice
45ml/3 tbsp low fat fromage frais
1 cooked chicken breast without skin,
    about 175g/6oz
4 large pittas or 8 small pittas
salt and black pepper
chopped fresh parsley, to garnish

1 Remove the tough central spine from the cabbage leaves, then finely shred the leaves using a large sharp knife. Place the shredded cabbage in a bowl and stir in the onion, radishes, apple and lemon juice.

2 Stir the fromage frais into the shredded cabbage mixture and season well with salt and pepper. Thinly slice the cooked chicken breast and stir into the shredded cabbage mixture until well coated in fromage frais.

3 Warm the pittas under a hot grill, then split them along one edge using a round-bladed knife. Spoon the filling into the pittas, then garnish with chopped fresh parsley.

COOK'S TIP
If the filled pittas need to be made more than an hour in advance, line the pitta breads with crisp lettuce leaves before adding the filling.

NUTRITION NOTES

Per portion:

Energy	232Kcals/976kJ
Fat	2.61g
Saturated fat	0.76g
Cholesterol	24.61mg
Fibre	2.97g

GRANARY SLTs

A quick, tasty snack or easy packed lunch with a healthy combination – sardines, lettuce and tomatoes!

INGREDIENTS

Serves 2

2 small Granary bread rolls
120g/4¼oz can sardines in olive oil
4 crisp green lettuce leaves, such as Webbs
1 beef tomato, sliced
juice of ½ lemon
salt and black pepper

1 Slice the bread rolls in half cross-ways using a sharp knife. Drain off the oil from the sardines into a small bowl, then brush the cut surfaces of the rolls with a small amount of the oil.

2 Cut or break the sardines into small pieces, then fill each roll with a lettuce leaf, some sliced tomato and pieces of sardine, sprinkling the filling with a little lemon juice, and salt and pepper to taste.

3 Sandwich the rolls back together and press the lids down lightly with your hand. Serve at once.

NUTRITION NOTES

Per portion:

Energy	248Kcals/1042kJ
Fat	8.51g
Saturated fat	1.86g
Cholesterol	32.5mg
Fibre	3.01g

COOK'S TIP
If you prefer to use sardines in tomato sauce, spread the bread rolls thinly with low fat spread before adding the filling.

TUNA CHILLI TACOS

Tacos are a useful, quick snack – but you will need to use both hands to eat them!

INGREDIENTS

Makes 8

8 taco shells
400g/14oz can red kidney beans, drained
120ml/4 fl oz/½ cup low fat fromage frais
2.5ml/½ tsp chilli sauce
2 spring onions, chopped
1 tsp/5 ml chopped fresh mint
½ small crisp lettuce, shredded
425g/15oz can tuna fish chunks in brine, drained
50g/2oz/¾ cup grated reduced fat Cheddar cheese
8 cherry tomatoes, quartered
mint sprigs, to garnish

1 Warm the taco shells in a hot oven for a few minutes until crisp.

2 Mash the beans lightly with a fork, then stir in the fromage frais with the chilli sauce, onions and mint.

3 Fill the taco shells with the shredded lettuce, the bean mixture and tuna. Top the filled shells with the cheese and serve at once with the tomatoes, garnished with sprigs of mint.

NUTRITION NOTES

Per portion:

Energy	147Kcals/615kJ
Fat	2.42g
Saturated fat	1.13g
Cholesterol	29.69mg
Fibre	2.41g

POTATO SKINS WITH CAJUN DIP

No need to deep fry potato skins for this treat – grilling crisps them up in no time.

INGREDIENTS

Serves 2

2 large baking potatoes
120g/4fl oz/½ cup natural yogurt
1 garlic clove, crushed
5ml/1 tsp tomato purée
2.5ml/½ tsp green chilli purée (or ½ small green chilli, chopped
1.25ml/¼ tsp celery salt
salt and black pepper

1 Bake or microwave the potatoes until tender. Cut them in half and scoop out the flesh, leaving a thin layer on the skins. Keep the scooped out potato for another meal.

2 Cut each potato in half again then place the pieces skin-side down on a large baking sheet.

3 Grill for 4–5 minutes, or until crisp. Mix together the dip ingredients and serve with the potato skins.

NUTRITION NOTES

Per portion:

Energy	202Kcals/847kJ
Fat	0.93g
Saturated fat	0.34g
Cholesterol	2.3mg
Fibre	3.03g

CHINESE GARLIC MUSHROOMS

Tofu is high in protein and very low in fat, so it is a very useful food to keep handy for quick meals and snacks like this one.

INGREDIENTS

Serves 4
8 large open mushrooms
3 spring onions, sliced
1 garlic clove, crushed
30ml/2 thsp oyster sauce
285g/10 oz packet marinated tofu, cut into small dice
200g/7oz can sweetcorn, drained
10ml/2 tsp sesame oil
salt and black pepper

1 Preheat the oven to 200°C/400°F/ Gas 6. Finely chop the mushroom stalks and mix with the spring onions, garlic and oyster sauce.

2 Stir in the diced marinated tofu and sweetcorn, season well with salt and pepper, then spoon the filling into the mushrooms.

3 Brush the edges of the mushrooms with the sesame oil. Arrange the stuffed mushrooms in a baking dish and bake for 12–15 minutes, until the mushrooms are just tender, then serve at once.

COOK'S TIP
If you prefer, omit the oyster sauce and use light soy sauce instead.

NUTRITION NOTES

Per portion:
Energy	137Kcals/575kJ
Fat	5.6g
Saturated fat	0.85g
Cholesterol	0
Fibre	1.96g

SURPRISE SCOTCH 'EGGS'

This reduced fat version of Scotch eggs is great for packed lunches or picnics. If half fat sausagemeat isn't available, buy half fat sausages or turkey sausages and remove the skins.

INGREDIENTS

Makes 3

75ml/5 tbsp chopped parsley and
  snipped chives, mixed
115g/4oz/½ cup skimmed milk soft
  cheese
450g/1 lb half fat sausagemeat
50g/2oz /½ cup rolled oats
salt and black pepper
mixed leaf and tomato salad, to serve

1 Preheat the oven to 200°C/400°F/ Gas 6. Mix together the herbs, cheese and seasonings, then roll into three even-sized balls.

2 Divide the sausagemeat into three and press each piece out to a round, about 1cm/½ in thick.

3 Wrap each cheese ball in a piece of sausagemeat, smoothing over all the joins to enclose the cheese completely. Spread out the rolled oats on a plate and roll the balls in the oats, using your hands to coat them evenly.

4 Place the balls on a baking sheet and bake for 30–35 minutes or until golden. Serve hot or cold, with a mixed leaf and tomato salad.

NUTRITION NOTES

Per portion:

Energy	352Kcals/1476kJ
Fat	15.94g
Saturated fat	0.29g
Cholesterol	66.38mg
Fibre	3.82g

SALMON PARCELS

Serve these little savoury parcels just as they are for a snack, or with a pool of fresh tomato sauce for a special starter.

───── INGREDIENTS ─────

Makes 12
90g/3½oz can red or pink salmon
15ml/1 tbsp chopped fresh coriander
4 spring onions, finely chopped
4 sheets filo pastry
sunflower oil, for brushing
spring onions and salad leaves, to
    serve

COOK'S TIP
When you are using filo pastry, it is important to prevent it drying out; cover any you are not using with a tea towel or cling film.

---

1 Preheat the oven to 200°C/400°F/ Gas 6. Lightly oil a baking sheet. Drain the salmon, discarding any skin and bones, then place in a bowl.

2 Flake the salmon with a fork and mix with the fresh coriander and spring onions.

3 Place a single sheet of filo pastry on a work surface and brush lightly with oil. Place another sheet on top. Cut into six squares, about 10cm/4in. Repeat with the remaining pastry, to make 12 squares.

4 Place a spoonful of the salmon mixture on to each square. Brush the edges of the pastry with oil, then draw together, pressing to seal. Place the pastries on a baking sheet and bake for 12–15 minutes, until golden. Serve warm, with spring onions and salad.

NUTRITION NOTES	
Per portion:	
Energy	25Kcals/107kJ
Fat	1.16g
Saturated fat	0.23g
Cholesterol	2.55mg
Fibre	0.05g

TOMATO CHEESE TARTS

These crisp little tartlets are easier to make than they look. Best eaten fresh from the oven.

───── INGREDIENTS ─────

Serves 4
2 sheets filo pastry
1 egg white
115g/4oz/½ cup skimmed milk soft
    cheese
handful fresh basil leaves
3 small tomatoes, sliced
salt and black pepper

1 Preheat the oven to 200°C/400°F/ Gas 6. Brush the sheets of filo pastry lightly with egg white and cut into sixteen 10 cm/4 in squares.

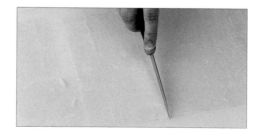

2 Layer the squares in twos, in eight patty tins. Spoon the cheese into the pastry cases. Season with black pepper and top with basil leaves.

3 Arrange tomatoes on the tarts, add seasoning and bake for 10-12 minutes, until golden. Serve warm.

NUTRITION NOTES	
Per portion:	
Energy	50Kcals/210kJ
Fat	0.33g
Saturated fat	0.05g
Cholesterol	0.29mg
Fibre	0.25g

Aubergine Sunflower Pâté

INGREDIENTS

Serves 4
1 large aubergine
1 garlic clove, crushed
15ml/1 tbsp lemon juice
30ml/2 tbsp sunflower seeds
45ml/3 tbsp natural low fat yogurt
handful fresh coriander or parsley
black pepper
black olives, to garnish

1 Cut the aubergine in half and place, cut side down, on a baking sheet. Place under a hot grill for 15–20 minutes, until the skin is blackened and the flesh is soft. Leave for a few minutes, to cool slightly.

2 Scoop the flesh of the aubergine into a food processor. Add the garlic, lemon juice, sunflower seeds and yogurt. Process until smooth.

3 Roughly chop the fresh coriander or parsley and mix in. Season, then spoon into a serving dish. Top with olives and serve with vegetable sticks.

NUTRITION NOTES	
Per portion:	
Energy	71Kcals/298kJ
Fat	4.51g
Saturated fat	0.48g
Cholesterol	0.45mg
Fibre	2.62g

Pepper Dips with Crudités

Make one or both of these colourful vegetable dips – if you have time to make both they look spectacular together.

INGREDIENTS

Serves 4–6
2 medium red peppers, halved and seeded
2 medium yellow peppers, halved and seeded
2 garlic cloves
30ml/2 tbsp lemon juice
20ml/4 tsp olive oil
50g/2oz fresh white breadcrumbs
salt and black pepper
fresh vegetables, for dipping

1 Place the peppers in separate saucepans with a peeled clove of garlic. Add just enough water to cover.

2 Bring to the boil, then cover and simmer for 15 minutes until tender. Drain, cool, then purée separately in a food processor or blender, adding half the lemon juice and olive oil to each.

3 Stir half the breadcrumbs into each and season to taste with salt and pepper. Serve the dips with a selection of fresh vegetables for dipping.

NUTRITION NOTES	
Per portion:	
Energy	103Kcals/432kJ
Fat	3.7g
Saturated fat	0.47g
Cholesterol	0
Fibre	2.77g

MEAT DISHES

There's no reason why meat should not be a valuable part of a low fat, low cholesterol diet, but you need to make careful choices when shopping, and adapt preparation and cooking methods to keep fats to a minimum. Remember that even lean meat has hidden fat, so grilling or roasting on a rack is an advantage, and any added fats should be low in saturates and used in moderation. A fat-trimmed roast needn't be dry, especially if you seal it with a moist, savoury crust as in Roast Pork in a Blanket. Even for casseroles, there's often no need to seal the meat in fat first – a non-stick pan will seal the meat in its own fat. Or choose stir-frying, which quickly seals the meat with just a touch of oil.

PORK AND CELERY POPOVERS

Lower in fat than they look, and a good way to make the meat go further, these little popovers will be popular with children.

INGREDIENTS

Serves 4

sunflower oil, for brushing
150g/5oz plain flour
1 egg white
250ml/8 fl oz/1 cup skimmed milk
120ml/4 fl oz/½ cup water
350g/12 oz lean minced pork
2 celery sticks, finely chopped
45ml/3 tbsp rolled oats
30ml/2 tbsp snipped chives
15ml/1 tbsp Worcestershire or brown sauce
salt and black pepper

1 Preheat the oven to 220°C/425°F/ Gas 7. Brush 12 deep patty tins with a very little oil.

2 Place the flour in a bowl and make a well in the centre. Add the egg white and milk and gradually beat in the flour. Gradually add the water, beating until smooth and bubbly.

3 Place the minced pork, celery, oats, chives, Worcestershire sauce and seasoning in a bowl and mix thoroughly. Mould the mixture into 12 small balls and place in the patty tins.

4 Cook for 10 minutes, remove from the oven and quickly pour the batter into the tins. Cook for a further 20–25 minutes, or until well risen and golden brown. Serve hot with thin gravy and fresh vegetables.

NUTRITION NOTES

Per portion:

Energy	344Kcals/1443kJ
Fat	9.09g
Saturated fat	2.7g
Cholesterol	61.62mg
Fibre	2.37g

BEEF AND MUSHROOM BURGERS

It's worth making your own burgers to cut down on fat – in these the meat is extended with mushrooms for extra fibre.

INGREDIENTS

Serves 4

1 small onion, chopped
150g/5oz/2 cups small cup mushrooms
450g/1 lb lean minced beef
50g/2oz/1 cup fresh wholemeal bread-
    crumbs
5ml/1 tsp dried mixed herbs
15ml/1 tbsp tomato purée
flour, for shaping
salt and black pepper

1 Place the onion and mushrooms in a food processor and process until finely chopped. Add the beef, bread-crumbs, herbs, tomato purée and seasonings. Process for a few seconds, until the mixture binds together but still has some texture.

2 Divide the mixture into 8–10 pieces, then press into burger shapes using lightly floured hands.

3 Cook the burgers in a non-stick frying pan, or under a hot grill for 12-15 minutes, turning once, until evenly cooked. Serve with relish and salad, in burger buns or pitta bread.

COOK'S TIP
The mixture is quite soft, so han-dle carefully and use a fish slice for turning to prevent the burgers from breaking up during cooking.

NUTRITION NOTES

Per portion

Energy	196Kcals/822kJ
Fat	5.9g
Saturated fat	2.21g
Cholesterol	66.37mg
Fibre	1.60g

CURRIED LAMB AND LENTILS

This colourful curry is packed with protein and low in fat.

INGREDIENTS

Serves 4
8 lean, boneless lamb leg steaks, about
*   500g/1¼ lb total weight*
1 medium onion, chopped
2 medium carrots, diced
1 celery stick, chopped
15ml/1 tbsp hot curry paste
30ml/2 tbsp tomato purée
475ml/16 fl oz/2 cups stock
175g/6oz/1 cup green lentils
salt and black pepper
fresh coriander leaves, to garnish
boiled rice, to serve

1 In a large, non-stick pan, fry the lamb steaks without fat until browned, turning once.

2 Add the vegetables and cook for 2 minutes, then stir in the curry paste, tomato purée, stock and lentils.

3 Bring to the boil, cover and simmer gently for 30 minutes until tender. Add more stock, if necessary. Season and serve with coriander and rice.

NUTRITION NOTES

Per portion:

Energy	375Kcals/1575kJ
Fat	13.03g
Saturated fat	5.34g
Cholesterol	98.75mg
Fibre	6.11g

GOLDEN PORK AND APRICOT CASSEROLE

The rich golden colour and warm spicy flavour of this simple casserole make it ideal for chilly winter days.

INGREDIENTS

Serves 4
4 lean pork loin chops
1 medium onion, thinly sliced
2 yellow peppers, seeded and sliced
10ml/2 tsp medium curry powder
15ml/1 tbsp plain flour
250ml/8 fl oz/1 cup chicken stock
115g/4oz/⅔ cup dried apricots
30ml/2 tbsp wholegrain mustard
salt and black pepper

1 Trim the excess fat from the pork and fry without fat in a large, heavy or non-stick pan until lightly browned.

2 Add the onion and peppers to the pan and stir over a moderate heat for 5 minutes. Stir in the curry powder and the flour.

3 Add the stock, stirring, then add the apricots and mustard. Cover and simmer for 25–30 minutes, until tender. Adjust the seasoning and serve hot, with rice or new potatoes.

NUTRITION NOTES

Per portion:

Energy	289Kcals/1213kJ
Fat	10.03g
Saturated fat	3.23g
Cholesterol	82.8mg
Fibre	4.86g

COUNTRY PORK WITH PARSLEY COBBLER

This hearty casserole is a complete main course in one pot.

INGREDIENTS

Serves 4

*450g/1 lb boneless pork shoulder,
  diced
1 small swede, diced
2 carrots, sliced
2 parsnips, sliced
2 leeks, sliced
2 celery sticks, sliced
750ml/1¼ pint/3⅔ cups boiling beef
  stock
30ml/2 tbsp tomato purée
30ml/2 tbsp chopped fresh parsley
50g/2oz/¼ cup pearl barley
celery salt and black pepper*

For the topping

*150g/5oz/1 cup plain flour
5ml/1 tsp baking powder
90ml/6 tbsp low fat fromage frais
45ml/3 tbsp chopped fresh parsley*

1 Preheat the oven to 180°C/350°F/ Gas 4. Fry the pork without fat, in a non-stick pan until lightly browned.

2 Add the vegetables to the pan and stir over a medium heat until lightly coloured. Tip into a large casserole dish, then stir in the stock, tomato purée, parsley and pearl barley.

3 Season with celery salt and pepper, then cover and place in the oven for about 1–1¼ hours, until the pork and vegetables are tender.

4 For the topping, sift the flour and baking powder with seasoning, then stir in the fromage frais and parsley with enough cold water to mix to a soft dough. Roll out to about 1cm/½ in thickness and cut into 12–16 triangles.

5 Remove the casserole from the oven and raise the temperature to 220°C/ 425°F/Gas 7.

6 Arrange the triangles over the casserole, overlapping. Bake for 15–20 minutes, until well risen and golden.

NUTRITION NOTES

Per portion:

Energy	461Kcals/1936kJ
Fat	10.55g
Saturated fat	3.02g
Cholesterol	77.85mg
Fibre	9.44g

BEEF STRIPS WITH ORANGE AND GINGER

Stir-frying is one of the best ways to cook with the minimum of fat. It's also one of the quickest ways to cook, but you do need to choose tender meat.

INGREDIENTS

Serves 4

450g/1 lb lean beef rump, fillet or sirloin, cut into thin strips
finely grated rind and juice of 1 orange
15ml/1 tbsp light soy sauce
5ml/1 tsp cornflour
2.5cm/1in piece root ginger, finely chopped
10ml/2 tsp sesame oil
1 large carrot, cut into thin strips
2 spring onions, thinly sliced

1 Place the beef strips in a bowl and sprinkle over the orange rind and juice. If possible, leave to marinate for at least 30 minutes.

2 Drain the liquid from the meat and set aside, then mix the meat with the soy sauce, cornflour and ginger.

NUTRITION NOTES

Per portion:

Energy	175Kcals/730kJ
Fat	6.81g
Saturated fat	2.31g
Cholesterol	66.37mg
Fibre	0.67g

3 Heat the oil in a wok or large frying pan and add the beef. Stir-fry for 1 minute until lightly coloured, then add the carrot and stir-fry for a further 2–3 minutes.

4 Stir in the spring onions and reserved liquid, then cook, stirring, until boiling and thickened. Serve hot with rice noodles or plain boiled rice.

PAN-FRIED MEDITERRANEAN LAMB

The warm summery flavours of the Mediterranean are combined for a simple weekday meal.

INGREDIENTS

Serves 4

8 lean lamb cutlets
1 medium onion, thinly sliced
2 red peppers, seeded and sliced
400g/14oz can plum tomatoes
1 garlic clove, crushed
45ml/3 tbsp chopped fresh basil leaves
30ml/2 tbsp chopped black olives
salt and black pepper

1 Trim any excess fat from the lamb, then fry without fat in a non-stick pan until golden brown.

2 Add the onion and peppers to the pan. Cook, stirring, for a few minutes to soften, then add the plum tomatoes, garlic and basil.

3 Cover and simmer for 20 minutes or until the lamb is tender. Stir in the olives, season and serve hot with pasta.

NUTRITION NOTES

Per portion:

Energy	224Kcals/939kJ
Fat	10.17g
Saturated fat	4.32g
Cholesterol	79mg
Fibre	2.48g

BACON KOFTAS

These easy koftas are good for barbecues and summer grills, served with lots of salad.

INGREDIENTS

Serves 4

225g/8oz lean smoked back bacon, roughly chopped
75g/3oz/1½ cups fresh wholemeal breadcrumbs
2 spring onions, chopped
15ml/1 tbsp chopped fresh parsley
finely grated rind of 1 lemon
1 egg white
black pepper
paprika
lemon rind and fresh parsley leaves, to garnish

1 Place the bacon in a food processor with the breadcrumbs, spring onions, parsley, lemon rind, egg white and pepper. Process the mixture until it is finely chopped and begins to bind together. Alternatively, use a mincer.

2 Divide the bacon mixture into eight even-sized pieces and shape into long ovals around eight wooden or bamboo skewers.

3 Sprinkle the koftas with paprika and cook under a hot grill or on a barbecue for about 8–10 minutes, turning occasionally, until browned and cooked through. Garnish with lemon rind and parsley leaves, then serve hot with lemon rice and salad.

NUTRITION NOTES

Per portion:

Energy	128Kcals/538kJ
Fat	4.7g
Saturated fat	1.61g
Cholesterol	10.13mg
Fibre	1.33g

Lamb Pie with Mustard Thatch

A pleasant change from a classic shepherd's pie – healthier, too.

INGREDIENTS

Serves 4

750g/1½ lb old potatoes, diced
30ml/2 tbsp skimmed milk
15ml/1 tbsp wholegrain or French
   mustard
450g/1 lb lean minced lamb
1 onion, chopped
2 celery sticks, sliced
2 carrots, diced
150ml/¼ pint/⅔ cup beef stock
60ml/4 tbsp rolled oats
15ml/1 tbsp Worcestershire sauce
30ml/2 tbsp fresh chopped rosemary,
   or 10ml/2 tsp dried
salt and black pepper

1 Cook the potatoes in boiling, lightly salted water until tender. Drain and mash until smooth, then stir in the milk and mustard. Meanwhile, preheat the oven to 200°C/400°F/Gas 6.

2 Break up the lamb with a fork and fry without fat in a non-stick pan until lightly browned. Add the onion, celery and carrots to the pan and cook for 2–3 minutes, stirring.

3 Stir in the stock and rolled oats. Bring to the boil, then add the Worcestershire sauce and rosemary and season to taste with salt and pepper.

4 Turn the meat mixture into a 1.8 litre/3 pint/7 cup ovenproof dish and spread over the potato topping evenly, swirling with the edge of a knife. Bake for 30–35 minutes, or until golden. Serve hot with fresh vegetables.

NUTRITION NOTES

Per portion:
Energy	422Kcals/1770kJ
Fat	12.41g
Saturated fat	5.04g
Cholesterol	89.03mg
Fibre	5.07g

SAUSAGE BEANPOT WITH DUMPLINGS

Sausages needn't be totally banned on a low fat diet, but choose them carefully. If you are unable to find a reduced-fat variety, choose turkey sausages instead, and always drain off any fat during cooking.

INGREDIENTS

Serves 4
450g/1 lb half-fat sausages
1 medium onion, thinly sliced
1 green pepper, seeded and diced
1 small red chilli, sliced, or 2.5ml/½ tsp chilli sauce
400g/14oz can chopped tomatoes
250ml/8 fl oz/1 cup beef stock
425g/15oz can red kidney beans, drained
salt and black pepper

For the dumplings
275g/10oz/2½ cups plain flour
10ml/2 tsp baking powder
225g/8oz/1 cup cottage cheese

1 Fry the sausages without fat in a non-stick pan until brown. Add the onion and pepper. Stir in the chilli, tomatoes and stock; bring to the boil.

NUTRITION NOTES

Per portion:
Energy	574Kcals/2409kJ
Fat	13.09g
Saturated fat	0.15g
Cholesterol	52.31mg
Fibre	9.59g

2 Cover and simmer gently for 15–20 minutes, then add the beans and bring to the boil.

3 To make the dumplings, sift the flour and baking powder together and add enough water to mix to a firm dough. Roll out thinly and stamp out 16–18 rounds using a 7.5cm/3in cutter.

4 Place a small spoonful of cottage cheese on each round and bring the edges of the dough together, pinching to enclose. Arrange the dumplings over the sausages in the pan, cover the pan and simmer for 10–12 minutes, until the dumplings are well risen. Serve hot.

GREEK LAMB PIE

INGREDIENTS

Serves 4

sunflower oil, for brushing
450g/1 lb lean minced lamb
1 medium onion, sliced
1 garlic clove, crushed
400g/14oz can plum tomatoes
30ml/2 tbsp chopped fresh mint
5ml/1 tsp grated nutmeg
350g/12oz young spinach leaves
270g/10 oz packet filo pastry
5ml/1 tsp sesame seeds
salt and black pepper

1 Preheat the oven to 200°C/400°F/ Gas 6. Lightly oil a 22cm/8½ in round spring form tin.

2 Fry the mince and onion without fat in a non-stick pan until golden. Add the garlic, tomatoes, mint, nutmeg and seasoning. Bring to the boil, stirring. Simmer, stirring occasionally, until most of the liquid has evaporated.

3 Wash the spinach and remove any tough stalks, then cook in only the water clinging to the leaves for about 2 minutes, until wilted.

4 Lightly brush each sheet of filo pastry with oil and lay in overlapping layers in the tin, leaving enough over-hanging to wrap over the top.

5 Spoon in the meat and spinach, then wrap the pastry over to enclose, scrunching it slightly. Sprinkle with sesame seeds and bake for about 25–30 minutes, or until golden and crisp. Serve hot, with salad or vegetables.

NUTRITION NOTES

Per portion:

Energy	444Kcals/1865kJ
Fat	15.36g
Saturated fat	5.51g
Cholesterol	88.87mg
Fibre	3g

ROAST PORK IN A BLANKET

INGREDIENTS

Serves 4

1.5kg/3 lb lean pork loin joint
1 eating apple, cored and grated
40g/1½oz/¼ cup fresh breadcrumbs
30ml/2 tbsp chopped hazelnuts
15ml/1 tbsp Dijon mustard
15ml/1 tbsp snipped fresh chives
salt and black pepper

1 Cut the skin from the pork leaving a thin layer of fat.

2 Preheat the oven to 220°C/425°F/ Gas 7. Place the meat on a rack in a roasting tin, cover with foil and roast for 1 hour, then reduce the oven temperature to 180°C/350°F/Gas 4.

3 Mix together the apple, bread-crumbs, nuts, mustard, chives and seasoning. Remove the foil and spread the breadcrumb mixture over the fat surface of the meat.

4 Cook the pork for 45–60 minutes, or until the meat juices run clear. Serve in slices with a rich gravy.

NUTRITION NOTES

Per portion:

Energy	367Kcals/1540kJ
Fat	18.73g
Saturated fat	5.19g
Cholesterol	129.38mg
Fibre	1.5g

RUBY BACON CHOPS

This sweet, tangy sauce works well with lean bacon chops.

INGREDIENTS

Serves 4
1 ruby grapefruit
4 lean bacon loin chops
45ml/3 tbsp redcurrant jelly
black pepper

NUTRITION NOTES

Per portion:
Energy	215Kcals/904kJ
Fat	8.40g
Saturated fat	3.02g
Cholesterol	20.25mg
Fibre	0.81g

1 Cut away all the peel and pith from the grapefruit, using a sharp knife, and carefully remove the segments, catching the juice in a bowl.

2 Fry the bacon chops in a non-stick frying pan without fat, turning them once, until golden and cooked.

3 Add the reserved grapefruit juice and redcurrant jelly to the pan and stir until melted. Add the grapefruit segments, then season with pepper and serve hot with fresh vegetables.

JAMAICAN BEANPOT

If pumpkin is not available, use any other type of squash, or try swede instead. This recipe is a good one to double – or even treble – for a crowd.

INGREDIENTS

Serves 4
450g/1 lb braising steak, diced
1 small pumpkin, about 450g/1 lb
*   diced flesh*
1 medium onion, chopped
1 green pepper, seeded and sliced
15ml/1 tbsp paprika
2 garlic cloves, crushed
2.5ml/1 in piece fresh ginger root,
*   chopped*
400g/14oz can chopped tomatoes
115g/4oz baby corn cobs
250ml/8 fl oz/1 cup beef stock
425g/15oz can chick-peas, drained
425g/15oz can red kidney beans,
*   drained*
salt and black pepper

1 Fry the diced beef without fat in a large flameproof casserole, stirring to seal it on all sides.

2 Stir in the pumpkin, onion and pepper, cook for a further 2 minutes, then add the paprika, garlic and ginger.

3 Stir in the tomatoes, corn and stock, then bring to the boil. Cover and simmer for 40–45 minutes or until tender. Add the chick-peas and beans and heat thoroughly. Adjust the seasoning with salt and pepper to taste and serve hot with couscous or rice.

NUTRITION NOTES

Per portion:
Energy	357Kcals/1500kJ
Fat	8.77g
Saturated fat	2.11g
Cholesterol	66.37mg
Fibre	10.63g

POULTRY AND GAME

Poultry and game are obvious choices for a low fat diet, as they are mostly very low in fat, and much of the fat they do contain is low in saturates. Chicken, always a favourite choice for family meals, is endlessly versatile and economical, and is well suited to low fat cooking methods. Turkey, also low fat, is now available in so many different cuts that it's almost interchangeable with chicken, and turkey mince can take the place of beef in healthy, savoury bakes and pasta dishes. For a change, introduce game into family meals, as it is particularly low in saturated fat and just as simple to cook as chicken. Even high fat poultry such as duck can be cooked in new ways to reduce fat – and add to the flavour.

TURKEY PASTITSIO

A traditional Greek pastitsio is a rich, high fat dish made with beef mince, but this lighter version is just as tasty.

INGREDIENTS

Serves 4–6
450g/1 lb lean minced turkey
1 large onion, finely chopped
60ml/4 tbsp tomato purée
250ml/8 fl oz/1 cup red wine or stock
5ml/1 tsp ground cinnamon
300g/11oz/2½ cups macaroni
300ml/½ pint/1¼ cups skimmed milk
25g/1oz/2 tbsp sunflower margarine
25g/1oz/3 tbsp plain flour
5ml/1 tsp grated nutmeg
2 tomatoes, sliced
60ml/4 tbsp wholemeal breadcrumbs
salt and black pepper
green salad, to serve

1 Preheat the oven to 220°C/425°F/ Gas 7. Fry the turkey and onion in a non-stick pan without fat, stirring until lightly browned.

2 Stir in the tomato purée, red wine or stock and cinnamon. Season, then cover and simmer for 5 minutes.

3 Cook the macaroni in boiling, salted water until just tender, then drain. Layer with the meat mixture in a wide ovenproof dish.

4 Place the milk, margarine and flour in a saucepan and whisk over a moderate heat until thickened and smooth. Add the nutmeg, and salt and pepper to taste.

5 Pour the sauce evenly over the pasta and meat. Arrange the tomato slices on top and sprinkle lines of bread-crumbs over the surface.

6 Bake for 30–35 minutes, or until golden brown and bubbling. Serve hot with a green salad.

NUTRITION NOTES

Per portion:
Energy	566Kcals/2382kJ
Fat	8.97g
Saturated fat	1.76g
Cholesterol	57.06mg
Fibre	4.86g

TUSCAN CHICKEN

This simple peasant casserole has all the flavours of traditional Tuscan ingredients. The wine can be replaced by chicken stock.

INGREDIENTS

Serves 4
8 chicken thighs, skinned
5ml/1 tsp olive oil
1 medium onion, sliced thinly
2 red peppers, seeded and sliced
1 garlic clove, crushed
300ml/ ½ pint/1¼ cups passata
150ml/¼ pint/⅔ cup dry white wine
*large sprig fresh oregano, or 5ml/1 tsp
    dried oregano*
400g/14oz can cannelini beans, drained
45ml/3 tbsp fresh breadcrumbs
salt and black pepper

1 Fry the chicken in the oil in a non-stick or heavy pan until golden brown. Remove and keep hot. Add the onion and peppers to the pan and gently sauté until softened, but not brown. Stir in the garlic.

2 Add the chicken, passata, wine and oregano. Season well, bring to the boil then cover the pan tightly.

NUTRITION NOTES

Per portion:
Energy	248Kcals/1045kJ
Fat	7.53g
Saturated fat	2.06g
Cholesterol	73mg
Fibre	4.03g

3 Lower the heat and simmer gently, stirring occasionally for 30–35 minutes or until the chicken is tender and the juices run clear, not pink, when pierced with the point of a knife.

4 Stir in the cannelini beans and simmer for a further 5 minutes until heated through. Sprinkle with the breadcrumbs and cook under a hot grill until golden brown.

Moroccan Spiced Roast Poussin

Ingredients

Serves 4

75g/3oz/1 cup cooked long grain rice
1 small onion, chopped finely
finely grated rind and juice of 1 lemon
30ml/2 tbsp chopped mint
45ml/3 tbsp chopped dried apricots
30ml/2 tbsp natural yogurt
10ml/2 tsp ground turmeric
10ml/2 tsp ground cumin
2 x 450g/1lb poussin
salt and black pepper
lemon slices and mint sprigs, to garnish

1 Preheat the oven to 200°C/400°F/ Gas 6. Mix together the rice, onion, lemon rind, mint and apricots. Stir in half each of the lemon juice, yogurt, turmeric, cumin, and salt and pepper.

2 Stuff the poussin with the rice mixture at the neck end only. Any spare stuffing can be served separately. Place the poussin on a rack in a roasting tin.

3 Mix together the remaining lemon juice, yogurt, turmeric and cumin, then brush this over the poussin. Cover loosely with foil and cook in the oven for 30 minutes.

4 Remove the foil and roast for a further 15 minutes, or until golden brown and the juices run clear, not pink, when pierced.

5 Cut the poussin in half with a sharp knife or poultry shears, and serve with the reserved rice. Garnish with lemon slices and fresh mint.

Nutrition Notes	
Per portion:	
Energy	219Kcals/919kJ
Fat	6.02g
Saturated fat	1.87g
Cholesterol	71.55mg
Fibre	1.12g

Sticky Ginger Chicken

Ingredients

Serves 4

30ml/2 tbsp lemon juice
30ml/2 tbsp light muscovado sugar
5ml/1 tsp grated fresh ginger root
10ml/2 tsp soy sauce
8 chicken drumsticks, skinned
black pepper

Nutrition Notes	
Per portion:	
Energy	162Kcals/679kJ
Fat	5.58g
Saturated fat	1.84g
Cholesterol	73mg
Fibre	0.08g

1 Mix together the lemon juice, sugar, ginger, soy sauce and pepper.

2 With a sharp knife, slash the chicken drumsticks about three times through the thickest part, then toss the chicken in the glaze.

3 Cook the chicken on a hot grill or barbecue, turning occasionally and brushing with the glaze, until the chicken is golden and the juices run clear, not pink, when pierced. Serve on a bed of lettuce, with crusty bread.

TURKEY SPIRALS

These little spirals may look difficult, but they're very simple to make, and a very good way to pep up plain turkey.

INGREDIENTS

Serves 4

4 thinly sliced turkey breast steaks, about 90g/3½oz each
20ml/4 tsp tomato purée
15g/½oz/½ cup large basil leaves
1 garlic clove, crushed
15ml/1 tbsp skimmed milk
30ml/2 tbsp wholemeal flour
salt and black pepper
passata or fresh tomato sauce and pasta with fresh basil, to serve

1 Place the turkey steaks on a board. If too thick, flatten them slightly by beating with a rolling pin.

2 Spread each turkey breast steak with tomato purée, then top with a few leaves of basil, a little crushed garlic, and salt and pepper.

3 Roll up firmly around the filling and secure with a cocktail stick. Brush with milk and sprinkle with flour to coat lightly.

4 Place the spirals on a foil-lined grill-pan. Cook under a medium-hot grill for 15–20 minutes, turning them occasionally, until thoroughly cooked. Serve hot, sliced with a spoonful or two of passata or fresh tomato sauce and pasta, sprinkled with fresh basil.

> COOK'S TIP
> When flattening the turkey steaks with a rolling pin, place them between two sheets of cling film.

NUTRITION NOTES

Per portion:

Energy	123Kcals/518kJ
Fat	1.21g
Saturated fat	0.36g
Cholesterol	44.17mg
Fibre	0.87g

CARIBBEAN CHICKEN KEBABS

These kebabs have a rich, sunshine Caribbean flavour and the marinade keeps them moist without the need for oil. Serve with a colourful salad and rice.

INGREDIENTS

Serves 4

500g/1¼ lb boneless chicken breasts, skinned
finely grated rind of 1 lime
30ml/2 tbsp lime juice
15ml/1 tbsp rum or sherry
15ml/1 tbsp light muscovado sugar
5ml/1 tsp ground cinnamon
2 mangoes, peeled and cubed
rice and salad, to serve

1 Cut the chicken into bite-sized chunks and place in a bowl with the lime rind and juice, rum, sugar and cinnamon. Toss well, cover and leave to stand for 1 hour.

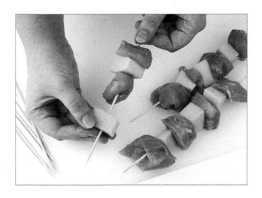

2 Save the juices and thread the chicken on to four wooden skewers, alternating with the mango cubes.

3 Cook the skewers under a hot grill or barbecue for 8–10 minutes, turning occasionally and basting with the juices, until the chicken is tender and golden brown. Serve at once with rice and salad.

COOK'S TIP
The rum or sherry adds a lovely rich flavour, but it is optional so can be omitted if you prefer to make the dish more economical.

NUTRITION NOTES

Per portion:

Energy	218Kcals/918kJ
Fat	4.17g
Saturated fat	1.33g
Cholesterol	53.75mg
Fibre	2.26g

CHILLI CHICKEN COUSCOUS

Couscous is a very easy alternative to rice and makes a good base for all kinds of ingredients.

INGREDIENTS

Serves 4
225g/8oz/2 cups couscous
1 litre/1¾ pint/4 cups boiling water
5ml/1 tsp olive oil
400g/14oz chicken without skin and bone, diced
1 yellow pepper, seeded and sliced
2 large courgettes, sliced thickly
1 small green chilli, thinly sliced, or 5ml/1 tsp chilli sauce
1 large tomato, diced
425g/15oz can chick-peas, drained
salt and black pepper
coriander or parsley sprigs to garnish

1 Place couscous in a large bowl and pour over boiling water. Cover and leave to stand for 30 minutes.

2 Heat the oil in a large, non-stick pan and stir fry the chicken quickly to seal, then reduce the heat.

3 Stir in the pepper, courgettes and chilli or sauce and cook for 10 minutes, until the vegetables are softened.

4 Stir in the tomato and chick-peas, then add the couscous. Adjust the seasoning and stir over a moderate heat until hot. Serve garnished with sprigs of fresh coriander or parsley.

NUTRITION NOTES

Per portion:
Energy	363Kcals/1525kJ
Fat	8.09g
Saturated fat	1.68g
Cholesterol	57mg
Fibre	4.38g

TURKEY BEAN BAKE

INGREDIENTS

Serves 4
1 medium aubergine, thinly sliced
15ml/1 tbsp olive oil, for brushing
450g/1 lb turkey breast, diced
1 medium onion, chopped
400g/14oz can chopped tomatoes
425g/15oz can red kidney beans, drained
15ml/1 tbsp paprika
15ml/1 tbsp fresh chopped thyme, or 5ml/1 tsp dried
5ml/1 tsp chilli sauce
350g/12oz/1½ cups Greek-style yogurt
2.5ml/½ tsp grated nutmeg
salt and black pepper

1 Preheat the oven to 190°C/375°F/ Gas 5. Arrange the aubergine in a colander and sprinkle with salt.

2 Leave the aubergine for 30 minutes, then rinse and pat dry. Brush a non-stick pan with oil and fry the aubergine in batches, turning once, until golden.

3 Remove aubergine, add the turkey and onion to the pan, then cook until lightly browned. Stir in the tomatoes, beans, paprika, thyme, chilli sauce, and salt and pepper. In a separate bowl, mix together the yogurt and grated nutmeg.

4 Layer the meat and aubergine in an ovenproof dish, finishing with aubergine. Spread over the yogurt and bake for 50–60 minutes, until golden.

NUTRITION NOTES

Per portion:
Energy	370Kcals/1555kJ
Fat	13.72g
Saturated fat	5.81g
Cholesterol	66.5mg
Fibre	7.38g

OAT-CRUSTED CHICKEN WITH SAGE

Oats make a good coating for savoury foods, and offer a good way to add extra fibre.

INGREDIENTS

Serves 4
45ml/3 tbsp skimmed milk
10ml/2 tsp English mustard
40g/1½ oz/½ cup rolled oats
45ml/3 tbsp chopped sage leaves
8 chicken thighs or drumsticks, skinned
115g/4oz/½ cup low fat fromage frais
5ml/1 tsp wholegrain mustard
salt and black pepper
fresh sage leaves, to garnish

1 Preheat the oven to 200°C/400°F/ Gas 6. Mix together the milk and English mustard.

2 Mix the oats with 30ml/2 tbsp of the sage and the seasoning on a plate. Brush the chicken with the milk and press into the oats to coat evenly.

3 Place the chicken on a baking sheet and bake for about 40 minutes, or until the juices run clear, not pink, when pierced through the thickest part.

4 Meanwhile, mix together the low fat fromage frais, mustard, remaining sage and seasoning, then serve with the chicken. Garnish the chicken with fresh sage and serve hot or cold.

COOK'S TIP
If fresh sage is not available, choose another fresh herb such as thyme or parsley, instead of using a dried alternative.

NUTRITION NOTES

Per portion:	
Energy	214Kcals/898kJ
Fat	6.57g
Saturated fat	1.81g
Cholesterol	64.64mg
Fibre	0.74g

CHICKEN IN CREAMY ORANGE SAUCE

This sauce is deceptively creamy – in fact it is made with low fat fromage frais, which is virtually fat-free. The brandy adds a richer flavour, but is optional – omit it if you prefer and use orange juice alone.

INGREDIENTS

Serves 4

8 chicken thighs or drumsticks, skinned
45ml/3 tbsp brandy
300ml/½ pint/1¼ cups orange juice
3 spring onions, chopped
10ml/2 tsp cornflour
90ml/6 tbsp low fat fromage frais
salt and black pepper

1 Fry the chicken pieces without fat in a non-stick or heavy pan, turning until evenly browned.

2 Stir in the brandy, orange juice and spring onions. Bring to the boil, then cover and simmer for 15 minutes, or until the chicken is tender and the juices run clear, not pink, when pierced.

3 Blend the cornflour with a little water then mix into the fromage frais. Stir this into the sauce and stir over a moderate heat until boiling.

4 Adjust the seasoning and serve with boiled rice or pasta and green salad.

COOK'S TIP
Cornflour stabilises the fromage frais and helps prevent it curdling.

NUTRITION NOTES

Per portion:

Energy	227Kcals/951kJ
Fat	6.77g
Saturated fat	2.23g
Cholesterol	87.83mg
Fibre	0.17g

MANDARIN SESAME DUCK

Duck is a high fat meat but it is possible to get rid of a good proportion of the fat cooked in this way. (If you remove the skin completely, the meat can be dry.) For a special occasion, duck breasts are a good choice, but they are more expensive.

INGREDIENTS

Serves 4

4 duck leg or boneless breast portions
30ml/2 tbsp light soy sauce
45ml/3 tbsp clear honey
15ml/1 tbsp sesame seeds
4 mandarin oranges
5ml/1 tsp cornflour
salt and black pepper

1 Preheat the oven to 180°C/350°F/ Gas 4. Prick the duck skin all over. Slash the breast skin diagonally at intervals with a sharp knife.

2 Place the duck on a rack in a roasting tin and roast for 1 hour. Mix 15ml/1 tbsp soy sauce with 30ml/2 tbsp honey and brush over the duck. Sprinkle with sesame seeds. Roast for 15–20 minutes, until golden brown.

3 Meanwhile, grate the rind from one mandarin and squeeze the juice from two. Mix in the cornflour, then stir in the remaining soy sauce and honey. Heat, stirring, until thickened and clear. Season. Peel and slice the remaining mandarins. Serve the duck, with the mandarin slices and the sauce.

NUTRITION NOTES

Per portion:

Energy	624Kcals/2621kJ
Fat	48.63g
Saturated fat	12.99g
Cholesterol	256mg
Fibre	0.95g

MINTY YOGURT CHICKEN

INGREDIENTS

Serves 4

8 chicken thigh portions, skinned
15ml/1 tbsp clear honey
30ml/2 tbsp lime or lemon juice
30ml/2 tbsp natural yogurt
60ml/4 tbsp chopped fresh mint
salt and black pepper

1 Slash the chicken flesh at intervals with a sharp knife. Place in a bowl.

2 Mix the lime or honey, lemon juice, yogurt, seasoning and half the mint.

3 Spoon the marinade over the chicken and leave to marinate for 30 minutes. Line the grill pan with foil and cook the chicken under a moderately hot grill until thoroughly cooked and golden brown, turning the chicken occasionally during cooking.

4 Sprinkle with remaining mint, serve with potatoes and tomato salad.

NUTRITION NOTES

Per portion:

Energy	171Kcals/719kJ
Fat	6.74g
Saturated fat	2.23g
Cholesterol	97.90mg
Fibre	0.01g

AUTUMN PHEASANT

Pheasant is worth buying as it is low in fat, full of flavour and never dry when cooked like this.

INGREDIENTS

Serves 4

1 oven-ready pheasant
2 small onions, quartered
3 celery sticks, thickly sliced
2 red eating apples, thickly sliced
120ml/4 fl oz/½ cup stock
15ml/1 tbsp clear honey
30ml/2 tbsp Worcestershire sauce
grated nutmeg
30ml/2 tbsp toasted hazelnuts
salt and black pepper

1 Preheat the oven to 180°C/350°F/ Gas 4. Fry the pheasant without fat in a non-stick pan, turning occasionally until golden. Remove and keep hot.

2 Fry the onions and celery in the pan to brown lightly. Spoon into a casserole and place the pheasant on top. Tuck the apple slices around it.

3 Spoon over the stock, honey and Worcestershire sauce. Sprinkle with nutmeg, salt and pepper, cover and bake for 1¼–1½ hours or until tender. Sprinkle with nuts and serve hot.

NUTRITION NOTES	
Per portion:	
Energy	387Kcals/1624kJ
Fat	16.97g
Saturated fat	4.28g
Cholesterol	126mg
Fibre	2.72g

CIDER BAKED RABBIT

Rabbit is a low fat meat and an economical choice for family meals. Chicken joints may be used as an alternative.

INGREDIENTS

Serves 4

450g/1 lb rabbit joints
15ml/1 tbsp plain flour
5ml/1 tsp dry mustard powder
3 medium leeks, thickly sliced
250ml/8 fl oz/1 cup dry cider
2 sprigs rosemary
salt and black pepper
fresh rosemary, to garnish

1 Preheat the oven to 180°C/350°F/ Gas 4. Place the rabbit joints in a bowl and sprinkle over the flour and mustard powder. Toss to coat evenly.

2 Arrange the rabbit in one layer in a wide casserole. Blanch the leeks in boiling water, then drain and add to the casserole.

3 Add the cider, rosemary and seasoning, cover, then bake for 1–1¼ hours, or until the rabbit is tender. Garnish with fresh rosemary and serve with jacket potatoes and vegetables.

NUTRITION NOTES	
Per portion:	
Energy	162Kcals/681kJ
Fat	4.22g
Saturated fat	1.39g
Cholesterol	62.13mg
Fibre	1.27g

FISH AND SEAFOOD

Fish is ideally designed for healthy, quick family meals. Most types of fish are very low in fat and high in protein, and even oily fish is high in essential fatty acids. Unlike meat, fish never needs long, slow cooking to tenderise it, so dinner can be on the table in less than half an hour! Tempt any reluctant fish eaters with wonderful exotic flavours – a spicy Moroccan Tagine perhaps, or a hearty Cod Creole to pep up the taste buds. Fussy young fish-eaters are sure to clear their plate of Hoki Balls in Tomato Sauce or Tuna and Corn Fish Cakes, or will even try mackerel if it is presented without risk of bones, on fun-to-eat kebabs.

HOKI BALLS IN TOMATO SAUCE

This quick meal is a good choice for young children, as you can guarantee no bones. If you like, add a dash of chilli sauce.

— INGREDIENTS —

Serves 4

450g/1 lb hoki or other white fish fillets, skinned

60ml/4 tbsp fresh wholemeal bread-crumbs

30ml/2 tbsp snipped chives or spring onion

400g/14oz can chopped tomatoes

50g/2oz/¾ cup button mushrooms, sliced

salt and black pepper

1 Cut the fish fillets into large chunks and place in a food processor. Add the wholemeal breadcrumbs, chives or spring onion. Season to taste with salt and pepper and process until the fish is finely chopped, but still has some texture left.

2 Divide the fish mixture into about 16 even-sized pieces, then mould them into balls with your hands.

3 Place the tomatoes and mushrooms in a wide saucepan and cook over a medium heat until boiling. Add the fish balls, cover and simmer for about 10 minutes, until cooked. Serve hot.

COOK'S TIP
Hoki is a good choice for this dish but if it's not available, use cod, haddock or whiting instead.

NUTRITION NOTES	
Per portion:	
Energy	138Kcals/580kJ
Fat	1.38g
Saturated fat	0.24g
Cholesterol	51.75mg
Fibre	1.89g

TUNA AND CORN FISH CAKES

These economical little tuna fish cakes are quick to make. Either use fresh mashed potatoes, or make a storecupboard version with instant mash.

INGREDIENTS

Serves 4

300g/11oz/1¼ cups cooked mashed
   potatoes
200g/7oz can tuna fish in soya oil,
   drained
115g/4oz/¾ cup canned or frozen
   sweetcorn
30ml/2 tbsp chopped fresh parsley
50g/2oz/1 cup fresh white or brown
   breadcrumbs
salt and black pepper
lemon wedges, to serve

1 Place the mashed potato in a bowl and stir in the tuna fish, sweetcorn and chopped parsley.

2 Season to taste with salt and pepper, then shape into eight patty shapes with your hands.

3 Spread out the breadcrumbs on a plate and press the fish cakes into the breadcrumbs to coat lightly, then place on a baking sheet.

4 Cook the fish cakes under a moderately hot grill until crisp and golden brown, turning once. Serve hot with lemon wedges and fresh vegetables.

COOK'S TIP
For simple storecupboard variations which are just as nutritious, try using canned sardines, red or pink salmon, or smoked mackerel in place of the tuna.

NUTRITION NOTES

Per portion:
Energy	203Kcals/852kJ
Fat	4.62g
Saturated fat	0.81g
Cholesterol	21.25mg
Fibre	1.82g

CRUNCHY-TOPPED COD

Colourful and quick to cook, this is ideal for weekday meals.

──────── INGREDIENTS ────────

Serves 4
4 pieces cod fillet, about 115g/4oz
each, skinned
2 medium tomatoes, sliced
50g/2oz/1 cup fresh wholemeal bread-
crumbs
30ml/2 tbsp chopped fresh parsley
finely grated rind and juice of ½ lemon
5 ml/1 tsp sunflower oil
salt and ground black pepper

1 Preheat the oven to 200°C/400°F/ Gas 6. Arrange the cod fillets in a wide, ovenproof dish.

2 Arrange the tomato slices on top. Mix together the breadcrumbs, fresh parsley, lemon rind and juice and the oil with seasoning to taste.

3 Spoon the crumb mixture evenly over the fish, then bake for 15–20 minutes. Serve hot.

NUTRITION NOTES	
Per portion:	
Energy	130Kcals/546kJ
Fat	2.06g
Saturated fat	0.32g
Cholesterol	52.9mg
Fibre	1.4g

SPECIAL FISH PIE

This fish pie is colourful, healthy and best of all very easy to make. For a more economical version, omit the prawns and replace with more fish fillet.

──────── INGREDIENTS ────────

Serves 4
350g/12oz haddock fillet, skinned
30ml/2 tbsp cornflour
115g/4oz cooked, peeled prawns
198g/7oz can sweetcorn, drained
75g/3oz frozen peas
150ml/¼ pint/⅔ cup skimmed milk
150g/5oz/⅔ cup low fat fromage frais
75g/3oz fresh wholemeal breadcrumbs
40g/1½oz/½ cup grated reduced fat
Cheddar cheese
salt and black pepper

1 Preheat the oven to 190°C/375°F/ Gas 5. Cut the haddock into bite-sized pieces and toss in cornflour to coat evenly.

2 Place the fish, prawns, sweetcorn and peas in an ovenproof dish. Beat together the milk, fromage frais and seasonings, then pour into the dish.

3 Mix together the breadcrumbs and grated cheese then spoon evenly over the top. Bake for 25–30 minutes, or until golden brown. Serve hot with fresh vegetables.

NUTRITION NOTES	
Per portion:	
Energy	290Kcals/1218kJ
Fat	4.87g
Saturated fat	2.1g
Cholesterol	63.91mg
Fibre	2.61g

HADDOCK AND BROCCOLI CHOWDER

A warming main-meal soup for hearty appetites.

INGREDIENTS

Serves 4
4 spring onions, sliced
450g/1 lb new potatoes, diced
300ml/½ pint/1¼ cups fish stock or
  water
300ml/½ pint/1¼ cups skimmed milk
1 bay leaf
225g/8oz/2 cups broccoli florets, sliced
450g/1 lb smoked haddock fillets,
  skinned
198g/7oz can sweetcorn, drained
black pepper
chopped spring onions, to garnish

1 Place the spring onions and potatoes in a large saucepan and add the stock, milk and bay leaf. Bring the soup to the boil, then cover the pan and simmer for 10 minutes.

2 Add the broccoli to the pan. Cut the fish into bite-sized chunks and add to the pan with the sweetcorn.

3 Season the soup well with black pepper, then cover the pan and simmer for a further 5 minutes, or until the fish is cooked through. Remove the bay leaf and scatter over the spring onion. Serve hot, with crusty bread.

COOK'S TIP
When new potatoes are not available, old ones can be used, but choose a waxy variety which will not disintegrate.

NUTRITION NOTES

Per portion:

Energy	268Kcals/1124kJ
Fat	2.19g
Saturated fat	0.27g
Cholesterol	57.75mg
Fibre	3.36g

MOROCCAN FISH TAGINE

Tagine is actually the name of the large Moroccan cooking pot used for this type of cooking, but you can use an ordinary casserole intead.

INGREDIENTS

Serves 4

2 garlic cloves, crushed
30ml/2 tbsp ground cumin
30ml/2 tbsp paprika
1 small red chilli (optional)
30ml/2 tbsp tomato purée
60ml/4 tbsp lemon juice
4 cutlets of whiting or cod, about 175g/6oz each
350g/12oz tomatoes, sliced
2 green peppers, seeded and thinly sliced
salt and black pepper
chopped fresh coriander, to garnish

1 Mix together the garlic, cumin, paprika, chilli, tomato purée and lemon juice. Spread this mixture over the fish, then cover and chill for about 30 minutes to let the flavour penetrate.

2 Preheat the oven to 200°C/400°F/ Gas 6. Arrange half of the tomatoes and peppers in a baking dish.

3 Cover with the fish, in one layer, then arrange the remaining tomatoes and pepper on top. Cover the baking dish with foil and bake for about 45 minutes, until the fish is tender. Sprinkle with chopped coriander or parsley to serve.

COOK'S TIP
If you are preparing this dish for a dinner party, it can be assembled completely and stored in the fridge, ready to bake when needed.

NUTRITION NOTES

Per portion:

Energy	203Kcals/855kJ
Fat	3.34g
Saturated fat	0.29g
Cholesterol	80.5mg
Fibre	2.48g

Seafood Pilaf

This all-in-one-pan main course is a satisfying meal for any day of the week. For a special meal, substitute dry white wine for the orange juice.

INGREDIENTS

Serves 4

10ml/2 tsp olive oil
250g/9oz/1¼ cups long grain rice
5ml/1 tsp ground turmeric
1 red pepper, seeded and diced
1 small onion, finely chopped
2 medium courgettes, sliced
150g/5oz/2 cups button mushrooms,
    halved
350ml/12 fl oz/1½ cups fish or chicken
    stock
150ml/¼ pint/⅔ cup orange juice
350g/12oz white fish fillets
12 fresh mussels in the shell (or cooked
    shelled mussels)
salt and ground black pepper
grated rind of 1 orange, to garnish

1 Heat the oil in a large, non-stick pan and fry the rice and turmeric over a low heat for about 1 minute.

2 Add the pepper, onion, courgettes, and mushrooms. Stir in the stock and orange juice. Bring to the boil.

3 Reduce the heat and add the fish. Cover and simmer gently for about 15 minutes, until the rice is tender and the liquid absorbed. Stir in the mussels and heat thoroughly. Adjust the seasoning, sprinkle with orange rind and serve hot.

NUTRITION NOTES

Per portion:

Energy	370Kcals/1555kJ
Fat	3.84g
Saturated fat	0.64g
Cholesterol	61.25mg
Fibre	2.08g

Salmon Pasta with Parsley Sauce

INGREDIENTS

Serves 4

450g/1 lb salmon fillet, skinned
225g/8oz/3 cups pasta, such as penne
    or twists
175g/6oz cherry tomatoes, halved
150ml/¼ pint/⅔ cup low fat crème
    fraîche
45ml/3 tbsp finely chopped parsley
finely grated rind of ½ orange
salt and black pepper

NUTRITION NOTES

Per portion:

Energy	452Kcals/1902kJ
Fat	17.4g
Saturated fat	5.36g
Cholesterol	65.63mg
Fibre	2.56g

1 Cut the salmon into bite-sized pieces, arrange on a heatproof plate and cover with foil.

2 Bring a large pan of salted water to the boil, add the pasta and return to the boil. Place the plate of salmon on top and simmer for 10–12 minutes, until the pasta and salmon are cooked.

3 Drain the pasta and toss with the tomatoes and salmon. Mix together the crème fraîche, parsley, orange rind and pepper to taste, then toss into the salmon and pasta and serve hot or cold.

STUFFED PLAICE ROLLS

Plaice fillets are a good choice for families because they are economical, easy to cook and free of bones. If you prefer, the skin can be removed first.

INGREDIENTS

Serves 4

1 medium courgette, grated
2 medium carrots, grated
60ml/4 tbsp fresh wholemeal breadcrumbs
15ml/1 tbsp lime or lemon juice
4 plaice fillets
salt and black pepper

1 Preheat the oven to 200°C/400°F/ Gas 6. Mix together the carrots and courgettes. Stir in the breadcrumbs, lime juice and seasoning.

2 Lay the fish fillets skin side up and divide the stuffing between them, spreading it evenly.

3 Roll up to enclose the stuffing and place in an ovenproof dish. Cover and bake for about 30 minutes, or until the fish flakes easily. Serve hot with new potatoes.

COOK'S TIP
This recipe creates its own delicious juices, but for an extra sauce, stir chopped fresh parsley into a little low fat fromage frais and serve with the fish.

NUTRITION NOTES

Per portion:

Energy	158Kcals/665kJ
Fat	3.22g
Saturated fat	0.56g
Cholesterol	50.4mg
Fibre	1.94g

MACKEREL KEBABS WITH PARSLEY DRESSING

Oily fish such as mackerel are ideal for grilling as they cook quickly and need no extra oil.

INGREDIENTS

Serves 4

450g/1 lb mackerel fillets
finely grated rind and juice of 1 lemon
45ml/3 tbsp chopped fresh parsley
12 cherry tomatoes
8 pitted black olives
salt and black pepper

1 Cut the fish into 4cm/1½in chunks and place in a bowl with half the lemon rind and juice, half of the parsley and some seasoning. Cover the bowl and leave to marinate for 30 minutes.

2 Thread the chunks of fish on to eight long wooden or metal skewers, alternating them with the cherry tomatoes and olives. Cook the kebabs under a hot grill for 3–4 minutes, turning the kebabs occasionally, until the fish is cooked.

3 Mix the remaining lemon rind and juice with the remaining parsley in a small bowl, then season to taste with salt and pepper. Spoon the dressing over the kebabs and serve hot with plain boiled rice or noodles and a leafy green salad.

COOK'S TIP
When using wooden or bamboo kebab skewers, soak them first in a bowl of cold water for a few minutes to help prevent them burning.

NUTRITION NOTES

Per portion:

Energy	268Kcals/1126kJ
Fat	19.27g
Saturated fat	4.5g
Cholesterol	61.88mg
Fibre	1g

OATY HERRINGS WITH RED SALSA

Herrings are one of the most economical and nutritious fish. If you buy them ready filleted, they're much easier to eat than the whole fish.

INGREDIENTS

Serves 4
30ml/2 tbsp skimmed milk
10ml/2 tsp Dijon mustard
2 large herrings, filletted
50g/2oz/⅔ cup rolled oats
salt and black pepper

For the salsa
1 small red pepper, seeded
4 medium tomatoes
1 spring onion, chopped
15ml/1 tbsp lime juice
5ml/1 tsp caster sugar

1 Preheat the oven to 200°C/400°F/ Gas 6. To make the salsa, place the pepper, tomatoes, spring onion, lime juice, sugar and seasoning in a food processor. Process until finely chopped.

2 Mix the milk and mustard, and the oats and pepper. Dip fillets into the mustard mixture, then oats to coat.

3 Place on a baking sheet, then bake for 20 minutes. Serve with the salsa.

NUTRITION NOTES	
Per portion:	
Energy	261Kcals/1097kJ
Fat	15.56g
Saturated fat	3.17g
Cholesterol	52.65mg
Fibre	2.21g

SPICED RAINBOW TROUT

Farmed rainbow trout are very good value and cook very quickly on a grill or barbecue. Herring and mackerel can be cooked in this way too.

INGREDIENTS

Serves 4
4 large rainbow trout fillets (about 150g/5oz each)
15ml/1 tbsp ground coriander
1 garlic clove, crushed
30ml/2 tbsp finely chopped fresh mint
5ml/1 tsp paprika
175g/6oz/¾ cup natural yogurt
salad and pitta bread, to serve

1 With a sharp knife, slash the flesh of the fish fillets through the skin fairly deeply at intervals.

2 Mix together the coriander, garlic, mint, paprika and yogurt. Spread this mixture evenly over the fish and leave to marinate for about an hour.

3 Cook the fish under a moderately hot grill or on a barbecue, turning occasionally, until crisp and golden. Serve hot with a crisp salad and some warmed pitta bread.

> COOK'S TIP
> If you are using the grill, it is best to line the grill pan with foil before cooking the trout.

NUTRITION NOTES	
Per portion:	
Energy	188Kcals/792kJ
Fat	5.66g
Saturated fat	1.45g
Cholesterol	110.87mg
Fibre	0.05g

COD CREOLE

INGREDIENTS

Serves 4

450g/1 lb cod fillets, skinned
15ml/1 tbsp lime or lemon juice
10ml/2 tsp olive oil
1 medium onion, finely chopped
1 green pepper, seeded and sliced
2.5ml/½ tsp cayenne pepper
2.5ml/½ tsp garlic salt
400g/14oz can chopped tomatoes

NUTRITION NOTES

Per portion:

Energy	130Kcals/546kJ
Fat	2.61g
Saturated fat	0.38g
Cholesterol	51.75mg
Fibre	1.61g

1 Cut the cod fillets into bite-sized chunks and sprinkle with the lime or lemon juice.

2 In a large, non-stick pan, heat the olive oil and fry the onion and pepper gently until softened. Add the cayenne pepper and garlic salt.

3 Stir in the cod with the chopped tomatoes. Bring to the boil, then cover and simmer for about 5 minutes, or until the fish flakes easily. Serve with boiled rice or potatoes.

FIVE-SPICE FISH

Chinese mixtures of spicy, sweet and sour flavours are particularly successful with fish, and dinner is ready in minutes.

INGREDIENTS

Serves 4

4 white fish fillets, such as cod, haddock or hoki (about 175g/6oz each)
5ml/1 tsp Chinese five-spice powder
20ml/4 tsp cornflour
15ml/1 tbsp sesame or sunflower oil
3 spring onions, shredded
5ml/1 tsp finely chopped root ginger
150g/5oz button mushrooms, sliced
115g/4oz baby corn cobs, sliced
30ml/2 tbsp soy sauce
45ml/3 tbsp dry sherry or apple juice
5ml/1 tsp sugar
salt and black pepper

1 Toss the fish in the five-spice powder and cornflour to coat.

2 Heat the oil in a frying pan or wok and stir-fry the onions, ginger mushrooms and corn cobs for about 1 minute. Add the fish and cook for 2–3 minutes, turning once.

3 Mix together the soy sauce, sherry and sugar then pour over the fish. Simmer for 2 minutes, adjust the seasoning, then serve with noodles and stir-fried vegetables.

NUTRITION NOTES

Per portion:

Energy	213Kcals/893kJ
Fat	4.41g
Saturated fat	0.67g
Cholesterol	80.5mg
Fibre	1.08g

PASTA, PIZZAS AND GRAINS

Pasta, pizzas and grain dishes should be encouraged at family meals as they're mostly very healthy foods. Pasta and rice are particularly low in fat, and contain good amounts of protein, carbohydrate and vitamins. Pasta is endlessly versatile, from quick Spaghetti with Tuna Sauce for an easy family dinner, to a more unusual Spinach and Hazelnut Lasagne. You'll soon discover that pasta doesn't have to be smothered in heavy sauces to be tasty. Add variety to meals by introducing different grains, such as polenta, couscous or bulgur wheat, which are just as easy and healthy as rice, but will help to keep appetites lively.

LEMON AND HERB RISOTTO CAKE

This unusual rice dish can be served as a main course with salad, or as a satisfying side dish. It's also good served cold, and packs well for picnics.

INGREDIENTS

Serves 4

1 small leek, thinly sliced
600ml/1 pint/2½ cups chicken stock
225g/8oz/1 cup short grain rice
finely grated rind of 1 lemon
30ml/2 tbsp chopped fresh chives
30ml/2 tbsp chopped fresh parsley
75g/3oz/¾ cup grated mozzarella
   cheese
salt and black pepper
parsley and lemon wedges, to garnish

1 Preheat the oven to 200°C / 400°F/ Gas 6. Lightly oil a 22cm / 8½ in round, loose-bottomed cake tin.

2 Cook the leek in a large pan with 45ml/3 tbsp stock, stirring over a moderate heat, to soften. Add the rice and the remaining stock.

3 Bring to the boil. Cover the pan and simmer gently, stirring occasionally, for about 20 minutes, or until all the liquid is absorbed.

4 Stir in the lemon rind, herbs, cheese and seasoning. Spoon into the tin, cover with foil and bake for 30–35 minutes or until lightly browned. Turn out and serve in slices, garnished with parsley and lemon wedges.

COOK'S TIP
The best type of rice to choose for this recipe is the Italian round grain Arborio rice, but if it is not available, use pudding rice instead.

NUTRITION NOTES

Per portion:

Energy	280Kcals/1176kJ
Fat	6.19g
Saturated fat	2.54g
Cholesterol	12.19mg
Fibre	0.9g

RICE WITH SEEDS AND SPICES

A change from plain boiled rice, and a colourful accompaniment to serve with spicy curries or grilled meats. Basmati rice gives the best texture and flavour, but you can use ordinary long grain rice instead, if you prefer.

INGREDIENTS

Serves 4

5ml/1 tsp sunflower oil
2.5ml/½ tsp ground turmeric
6 cardamom pods, lightly crushed
5ml/1 tsp coriander seeds, lightly crushed
1 garlic clove, crushed
200g/7oz/1 cup basmati rice
400ml/14 fl oz/1⅔ cups stock
115g/4oz/½ cup natural yogurt
15ml/1 tbsp toasted sunflower seeds
15ml/1 tbsp toasted sesame seeds
salt and black pepper
coriander leaves, to garnish

1 Heat the oil in a non-stick pan and fry the spices and garlic for about 1 minute, stirring all the time.

2 Add the rice and stock, bring to the boil then cover and simmer for 15 minutes or until just tender.

3 Stir in the yogurt and the toasted sunflower and sesame seeds. Adjust the seasoning and serve hot, garnished with coriander leaves.

NUTRITION NOTES

Per portion:

Energy	243Kcals/1022kJ
Fat	5.5g
Saturated fat	0.73g
Cholesterol	1.15mg
Fibre	0.57g

COOK'S TIP
Seeds are particularly rich in minerals, so they are a good addition to all kinds of dishes. Light roasting will improve their flavour.

CORN GRIDDLE PANCAKES

These crisp pancakes are delicious to serve as a snack lunch, or as a light supper with a crisp mixed salad.

INGREDIENTS

Serves 4, makes about 12
115g/4oz/1 cup self-raising flour
1 egg white
150ml/¼ pint/⅔ cup skimmed milk
200g/7oz can sweetcorn, drained
oil, for brushing
salt and black pepper
tomato chutney, to serve

1 Place the flour, egg white and skimmed milk in a food processor or blender with half the sweetcorn and process until smooth.

2 Season the batter well and add the remaining sweetcorn.

3 Heat a frying pan and brush with oil. Drop in tablespoons of batter and cook until set. Turn over the pancakes and cook the other side until golden. Serve hot with tomato chutney.

NUTRITION NOTES

Per portion:
Energy	162Kcals/680kJ
Fat	0.89g
Saturated fat	0.14g
Cholesterol	0.75mg
Fibre	1.49g

BAKED POLENTA WITH TOMATOES

INGREDIENTS

Serves 4
750ml/1¼ pints/3⅔ cups stock
175g/6oz/1⅛ cup polenta (coarse corn-meal)
60ml/4 tbsp chopped fresh sage
5ml/1 tsp olive oil
2 beefsteak tomatoes, sliced
15ml/1 tbsp grated Parmesan cheese
salt and black pepper

1 Bring the stock to the boil in a large saucepan, then gradually stir in the polenta.

2 Continue stirring the polenta over a moderate heat for about 5 minutes, until the mixture begins to come away from the sides of the pan. Stir in the chopped sage and season well, then spoon into a lightly oiled, shallow 23 x 33cm/9x13 in tin and spread evenly. Leave to cool.

3 Preheat the oven to 200°C/400°F/Gas 6. Cut the cooled polenta into 24 squares using a sharp knife.

4 Arrange the polenta overlapping with tomato slices in a lightly oiled, shallow ovenproof dish. Sprinkle with Parmesan and bake for 20 minutes or until golden brown. Serve hot.

NUTRITION NOTES

Per portion:
Energy	200Kcals/842kJ
Fat	3.8g
Saturated fat	0.77g
Cholesterol	1.88mg
Fibre	1.71g

Bulgur and Lentil Pilaf

Bulgur wheat is very easy to cook and can be used in almost any way you would normally use rice, hot or cold. Some of the finer grades need hardly any cooking, so check the pack for cooking times.

Ingredients

Serves 4
5ml/1 tsp olive oil
1 large onion, thinly sliced
2 garlic cloves, crushed
5ml/1 tsp ground coriander
5ml/1 tsp ground cumin
5ml/1 tsp ground turmeric
2.5ml/½ tsp ground allspice
225g/8oz/1¼ cups bulgur wheat
about 750ml/1¼ pints/3⅔ cups stock or
   water
115g/4oz button mushrooms, sliced
115g/4oz/⅔ cup green lentils
salt, black pepper and cayenne

1 Heat the oil in a non-stick saucepan and fry the onion, garlic and spices for 1 minute, stirring.

2 Stir in the bulgur wheat and cook, stirring, for about 2 minutes, until lightly browned. Add the stock or water, mushrooms and lentils.

3 Simmer over a very low heat for about 25–30 minutes, until the bulgur wheat and lentils are tender and all the liquid is absorbed. Add more stock or water, if necessary.

4 Season well with salt, pepper and cayenne and serve hot.

Cook's Tip
Green lentils can be cooked without presoaking, as they cook quite quickly and keep their shape. However, if you have the time, soaking them first will shorten the cooking time slightly.

Nutrition Notes

Per portion:

Energy	325Kcals/1367kJ
Fat	2.8g
Saturated fat	0.33g
Cholesterol	0
Fibre	3.61g

MINTED COUSCOUS CASTLES

Couscous is a fine semolina made from wheat grain, which is usually steamed and served plain with a rich meat or vegetable stew. Here it is flavoured with mint and moulded to make an unusual accompaniment to serve with any savoury dish.

INGREDIENTS

Serves 6

225g/8oz/1¼ cups couscous
475ml/16 fl oz/2 cups boiling stock
15ml/1 tbsp lemon juice
2 tomatoes, diced
30ml/2 tbsp chopped fresh mint
oil, for brushing
salt and black pepper
mint sprigs, to garnish

1 Place the couscous in a bowl and pour over the boiling stock. Cover the bowl and leave to stand for 30 minutes, until all the stock is absorbed and the grains are tender.

2 Stir in the lemon juice with the tomatoes and chopped mint. Adjust the seasoning with salt and pepper.

3 Brush the insides of four cups or individual moulds with oil. Spoon in the couscous mixture and pack down firmly. Chill for several hours.

4 Turn out and serve cold, or alternatively, cover and heat gently in a low oven or microwave, then turn out and serve hot, garnished with mint.

COOK'S TIP
Most packet couscous is now the ready cooked variety, which can be cooked as above, but some types need steaming first, so check the pack instructions.

NUTRITION NOTES

Per portion:

Energy	95Kcals/397kJ
Fat	0.53g
Saturated fat	0.07g
Cholesterol	0
Fibre	0.29g

TAGLIATELLE WITH HAZELNUT PESTO

Hazelnuts are lower in fat than other nuts, which makes them useful for this reduced-fat alternative to pesto sauce.

INGREDIENTS

Serves 4

2 garlic cloves, crushed
25g/1oz/1 cup fresh basil leaves
25g/1oz/¼ cup hazelnuts
200g/7oz/⅞ cup skimmed milk soft cheese
225g/8oz dried tagliatelle, or 450g/1 lb fresh
salt and black pepper

1 Place the garlic, basil, hazelnuts and cheese in a food processor or blender and process to a thick paste.

2 Cook the tagliatelle in lightly salted boiling water until just tender, then drain well.

3 Spoon the sauce into the hot pasta, tossing until melted. Sprinkle with pepper and serve hot.

NUTRITION NOTES

Per portion:

Energy	274Kcals/1155kJ
Fat	5.05g
Saturated fat	0.43g
Cholesterol	0.5mg
Fibre	2.14g

SPAGHETTI WITH TUNA SAUCE

A speedy midweek meal, which can also be made with other pasta shapes.

INGREDIENTS

Serves 4

225g/8oz dried spaghetti, or 450g/1 lb fresh
1 garlic clove, crushed
400g/14oz can chopped tomatoes
425g/15oz can tuna fish in brine, flaked
2.5ml/½ tsp chilli sauce (optional)
4 pitted black olives, chopped
salt and black pepper

> COOK'S TIP
> If fresh tuna is available, use 450g/1lb, cut into small chunks, and add after step 2. Simmer for 6–8 minutes, then add the chilli, olives and pasta.

1 Cook the spaghetti in lightly salted boiling water for 12 minutes or until just tender. Drain well and keep hot.

2 Add the garlic and tomatoes to the saucepan and bring to the boil. Simmer, uncovered, for 2–3 minutes.

3 Add the tuna, chilli sauce, if using, the olives and spaghetti. Heat well, add the seasoning and serve hot.

NUTRITION NOTES

Per portion:

Energy	306Kcals/1288kJ
Fat	2.02g
Saturated fat	0.37g
Cholesterol	48.45mg
Fibre	2.46g

SPINACH AND HAZELNUT LASAGNE

A vegetarian dish which is hearty enough to satisfy meat-eaters too. Use frozen spinach if you're short of time.

INGREDIENTS

Serves 4
900g/2 lb fresh spinach
300ml/½ pint/1¼ cups vegetable or
    chicken stock
1 medium onion, finely chopped
1 garlic clove, crushed
75g/3oz/¾ cup hazelnuts
30ml/2 tbsp chopped fresh basil
6 sheets lasagne
400g/14oz can chopped tomatoes
200g/7oz/1 cup low fat fromage frais
flaked hazlenuts and chopped parsley,
    to garnish

1 Preheat the oven to 200°C/400°F/ Gas 6. Wash the spinach and place in a pan with just the water that clings to the leaves. Cook the spinach on a fairly high heat for 2 minutes until wilted. Drain well.

2 Heat 30ml/2 tbsp of the stock in a large pan and simmer the onion and garlic until soft. Stir in the spinach, hazelnuts and basil.

3 In a large ovenproof dish, layer the spinach, lasagne and tomatoes. Season well between the layers. Pour over the remaining stock. Spread the fromage frais over the top.

4 Bake the lasagne for about 45 minutes, or until golden brown. Serve hot, sprinkled with lines of flaked hazelnuts and chopped parsley.

COOK'S TIP
The flavour of hazelnuts is improved by roasting. Place them on a baking sheet and bake in a moderate oven, or under a hot grill, until light golden.

NUTRITION NOTES

Per portion:
Energy	365Kcals/1532kJ
Fat	17g
Saturated fat	1.46g
Cholesterol	0.5mg
Fibre	8.16g

CALZONE

Makes 4
450g/1 lb/4 cups plain flour
pinch of salt
1 sachet easy-blend yeast
about 350ml/12 fl oz/1½ cups warm
 water

For the filling
5ml/1 tsp olive oil
1 medium red onion, thinly sliced
3 medium courgettes, about 350g/12oz
 total weight, sliced
2 large tomatoes, diced
150g/5oz mozzarella cheese, diced
15ml/1 tbsp chopped fresh oregano
skimmed milk, to glaze
salt and black pepper

1 To make the dough, sift the flour and salt into a bowl and stir in the yeast. Stir in just enough warm water to mix to a soft dough.

2 Knead for 5 minutes until smooth. Cover and leave in a warm place for about 1 hour, or until doubled in size.

3 Meanwhile, to make the filling, heat the oil and sauté the onion and courgettes for 3–4 minutes. Remove from the heat and add the tomatoes, cheese, oregano and seasoning.

4 Preheat the oven to 220°C/425°F/ Gas 7. Knead the dough lightly and divide into four. Roll out each piece on a lightly floured surface to a 20cm/8in round and place a quarter of the filling on one half.

5 Brush the edges with milk and fold over to enclose the filling. Press firmly to enclose. Brush with milk.

6 Bake on an oiled baking sheet for 15–20 minutes. Serve hot or cold.

NUTRITION NOTES	
Per portion:	
Energy	544Kcals/2285kJ
Fat	10.93g
Saturated fat	5.49g
Cholesterol	24.42mg
Fibre	5.09g

PENNE WITH BROCCOLI AND CHILLI

INGREDIENTS

Serves 4

450g/1 lb small broccoli florets
30ml/2 tbsp stock
1 garlic clove, crushed
1 small red chilli pepper, sliced, or
   2.5ml/½ tsp chilli sauce
60ml/4 tbsp natural low fat yogurt
30ml/2 tbsp toasted pine nuts or
   cashews
350g/12oz/3¾ cups penne pasta
salt and black pepper

3 Stir in the broccoli, pasta and yogurt. Adjust the seasoning, sprinkle with nuts and serve hot.

2 Heat the stock and add the crushed garlic and chilli or chilli sauce. Stir over a low heat for 2–3 minutes.

1 Add the pasta to a large pan of lightly salted boiling water and return to the boil. Place the broccoli in a steamer basket over the top. Cover and cook for 8–10 minutes until both are just tender. Drain.

NUTRITION NOTES

Per portion:

Energy	403Kcals/1695kJ
Fat	7.87g
Saturated fat	0.89g
Cholesterol	0.6mg
Fibre	5.83g

CREOLE JAMBALAYA

INGREDIENTS

Serves 6

4 boneless chicken thighs, skinned and
   diced
1 large green pepper, seeded and sliced
3 celery sticks, sliced
4 spring onions, sliced
about 300ml/½ pint/1¼ cups chicken
   stock
400g/14oz can tomatoes
5ml/1 tsp ground cumin
5ml/1 tsp ground allspice
2.5ml/½ tsp cayenne pepper
5ml/1 tsp dried thyme
300g/10oz/1½ cups long grain rice
200g/7oz cooked, peeled prawns
salt and black pepper

3 Stir in the rice and stock. Cover closely and cook for about 20 minutes, stirring occasionally, until the rice is tender. Add more stock if necessary.

2 Add the pepper, celery and onions with 15ml/1 tbsp stock. Cook for a few minutes to soften, then add the tomatoes, spices and thyme.

4 Add the prawns and heat well. Season and serve with a crisp salad.

1 Fry the chicken in a non-stick pan without fat, turning occasionally, until golden brown.

NUTRITION NOTES

Per portion:

Energy	282Kcals/1185kJ
Fat	3.37g
Saturated fat	0.85g
Cholesterol	51.33mg
Fibre	1.55g

PASTA WITH PASSATA AND CHICK PEAS

INGREDIENTS

Serves 4

300g/10oz/2 cups pasta
5ml/1 tsp olive oil
1 small onion, finely chopped
1 garlic clove, crushed
1 celery stick, finely chopped
425g/15oz can chick-peas, drained
250ml/8 fl oz/1 cup passata
salt and black pepper
chopped fresh parsley, to garnish

1 Heat the olive oil in a non-stick pan and fry the onion, garlic and celery until softened but not browned. Stir in the chick-peas and passata, then cover and simmer for about 15 minutes.

2 Cook the pasta in a large pan of boiling, lightly salted water until just tender. Drain the pasta and toss into the sauce, then season to taste with salt and pepper. Sprinkle with chopped fresh parsley, then serve hot.

NUTRITION NOTES

Per portion:

Energy	374Kcals/1570kJ
Fat	4.44g
Saturated fat	0.32g
Cholesterol	0
Fibre	6.41g

PEPERONATA PIZZA

INGREDIENTS

Makes 2 large pizzas

450g/1 lb/4 cups plain flour
pinch of salt
1 sachet easy-blend yeast
*about 350ml/12 fl oz/1½ cups warm
    water*

For the topping

1 onion, sliced
10ml/2 tsp olive oil
*2 large red and 2 yellow peppers,
    seeded and sliced*
1 garlic clove, crushed
400g/14oz can tomatoes
8 pitted black olives, halved
salt and black pepper

NUTRITION NOTES

Per portion:

Energy	965Kcals/4052kJ
Fat	9.04g
Saturated fat	1.07g
Cholesterol	0
Fibre	14.51g

1 To make the dough, sift the flour and salt into a bowl and stir in the yeast. Stir in just enough warm water to mix to a soft dough.

2 Knead for 5 minutes until smooth. Cover and leave in a warm place for about 1 hour, or until doubled in size.

3 To make the topping, fry the onion in the oil until soft, then stir in the peppers, garlic and tomatoes. Cover and simmer for 30 minutes, until no free liquid remains. Season to taste.

4 Preheat the oven to 230°C/450°F/ Gas 8. Divide the dough in half and press out each piece on a lightly oiled baking sheet to a 28cm/11in round, turning up the edges slightly.

5 Spread over the topping, dot with olives and bake for 15–20 minutes. Serve hot or cold with salad.

VEGETABLES AND SALADS

We're very lucky to have a huge variety of fresh vegetables available all year round these days, so there is no excuse for not making maximum use of them in every meal, whether they form the basis of the main course, or are served as an accompaniment to meat or fish dishes. Get out of that dull daily rut of the same old familiar vegetables and try pepping them up with unusual flavours – Brussels sprouts will never be the same again when you've cooked them Chinese-style, and if you thought roast potatoes were banned, try Rosemary Roasties. Take a fresh look at salads, too, and discover that they needn't be soaked in heavy, oily dressings. Tangy natural low fat yogurt dressings or mustard and honey mixtures are light, flavourful and low in fat.

CHINESE SPROUTS

If you are bored with plain boiled Brussels sprouts, try pepping them up with this unusual stir-fried method, which uses the minimum of oil.

INGREDIENTS

Serves 4

450g/1 lb Brussels sprouts, shredded
5ml/1 tsp sesame or sunflower oil
2 spring onions, sliced
2.5ml/½ tsp Chinese five-spice powder
15ml/1 tbsp light soy sauce

1 Trim the Brussels sprouts, then shred them finely using a large sharp knife or shred in a food processor.

2 Heat the oil and add the sprouts and onions, then stir-fry for about 2 minutes, without browning.

3 Stir in the five-spice powder and soy sauce, then cook, stirring, for a further 2–3 minutes, until just tender.

4 Serve hot, with grilled meats or fish, or Chinese dishes.

COOK'S TIP
Brussels sprouts are rich in Vitamin C, and this is a good way to cook them to preserve the vitamins. Larger sprouts cook particularly well by this method, and cabbage can also be cooked this way.

NUTRITION NOTES

Per portion:

Energy	58Kcals/243kJ
Fat	2.38g
Saturated fat	0.26g
Cholesterol	0
Fibre	4.67g

LEMONY VEGETABLE PARCELS

INGREDIENTS

Serves 4

2 medium carrots
1 small swede
1 large parsnip
1 leek, sliced
finely grated rind of ½ lemon
15ml/1 tbsp lemon juice
15ml/1 tbsp wholegrain mustard
5ml/1 tsp walnut or sunflower oil
salt and black pepper

1 Preheat the oven to 190°C/375°F/ Gas 5. Peel the root vegetables and cut into 1cm/½ in cubes. Place in a large bowl, then add the sliced leek.

2 Stir the lemon rind and juice and the mustard into the vegetables and mix well, then season to taste.

3 Cut four 30cm/12 in squares of non-stick baking paper and brush lightly with the oil.

4 Divide the vegetables among them. Roll up the paper from one side, then twist the ends firmly to seal.

5 Place the parcels on a baking sheet and bake for 50–55 minutes, or until the vegetables are just tender. Serve hot with roast or grilled meats.

NUTRITION NOTES

Per portion

Energy	78Kcals/326kJ
Fat	2.06g
Saturated fat	0.08g
Cholesterol	0
Fibre	5.15g

VEGETABLE RIBBONS

This may just tempt a few fussy eaters to eat up their vegetables!

INGREDIENTS

Serves 4
3 medium carrots
3 medium courgettes
120ml/4 fl oz/½ cup chicken stock
30ml/2 tbsp chopped fresh parsley
salt and black pepper

1 Using a vegetable peeler or sharp knife, cut the carrots and courgettes into thin ribbons.

2 Bring the stock to the boil in a large saucepan and add the carrots. Return the stock to the boil, then add the courgettes. Boil rapidly for 2–3 minutes, or until the vegetable ribbons are just tender.

3 Stir in the parsley, season lightly and serve hot.

NUTRITION NOTES	
Per portion:	
Energy	35Kcals/144kJ
Fat	0.53g
Saturated fat	0.09g
Cholesterol	0
Fibre	2.19g

VEGGIE BURGERS

INGREDIENTS

Serves 4
115g/4oz cup mushrooms, finely
  chopped
1 small onion, chopped
1 small courgette, chopped
1 carrot, chopped
25g/1oz unsalted peanuts or cashews
115g/4oz/2 cups fresh breadcrumbs
30ml/2 tbsp chopped fresh parsley
5ml/1 tsp yeast extract
salt and black pepper
fine oatmeal or flour, for shaping

1 Cook the mushrooms in a non-stick pan without oil, stirring, for 8–10 minutes to drive off all the moisture.

2 Process the onion, courgette, carrot and nuts in a food processor until beginning to bind together.

3 Stir in the mushrooms, breadcrumbs, parsley, yeast extract and seasoning to taste. With the oatmeal or flour, shape into four burgers. Chill.

4 Cook the burgers in a non-stick frying pan with very little oil or under a hot grill for 8–10 minutes, turning once, until the burgers are cooked and golden brown. Serve hot with a crisp salad.

NUTRITION NOTES	
Per portion:	
Energy	126Kcals/530kJ
Fat	3.8g
Saturated fat	0.73g
Cholesterol	0
Fibre	2.21g

MIDDLE-EASTERN VEGETABLE STEW

A spiced dish of mixed vegetables which can be served as a side dish or as a vegetarian main course. Children may prefer less chilli.

INGREDIENTS

Serves 4–6
45ml/3 tbsp vegetable or chicken stock
1 green pepper, seeded and sliced
2 medium courgettes, sliced
2 medium carrots, sliced
2 celery sticks, sliced
2 medium potatoes, diced
400g/14oz can chopped tomatoes
5ml/1 tsp chilli powder
30ml/2 tbsp chopped fresh mint
15ml/1 tbsp ground cumin
400g/14oz can chick-peas, drained
salt and black pepper
mint sprigs, to garnish

1 Heat the vegetable or chicken stock in a large flameproof casserole until boiling, then add the sliced pepper, courgettes, carrot and celery. Stir over a high heat for 2–3 minutes, until the vegetables are just beginning to soften.

2 Add the potatoes, tomatoes, chilli powder, mint and cumin. Add the chick-peas and bring to the boil.

3 Reduce the heat, cover the casserole and simmer for 30 minutes, or until all the vegetables are tender. Season to taste with salt and pepper and serve hot garnished with mint leaves.

COOK'S TIP
Chick-peas are traditional in this type of Middle-Eastern dish, but if you prefer, red kidney beans or haricot beans can be used instead.

NUTRITION NOTES
Per portion:	
Energy	168Kcals/703kJ
Fat	3.16g
Saturated fat	0.12g
Cholesterol	0
Fibre	6.13g

SUMMER VEGETABLE BRAISE

Tender, young vegetables are ideal for quick cooking in a minimum of liquid. Use any mixture of the family's favourite vegetables, as long as they are of similar size.

INGREDIENTS

Serves 4

175g/6oz/2½ cups baby carrots
175g/6oz/2 cups sugar-snap peas or
  mangetout
115g/4oz/1¼ cups baby corn cobs
90ml/6 tbsp vegetable stock
10ml/2 tsp lime juice
salt and black pepper
chopped fresh parsley parsley and
  snipped fresh chives, to garnish

1 Place the carrots, peas and baby corn cobs in a large heavy-based saucepan with the vegetable stock and lime juice. Bring to the boil.

2 Cover the pan and reduce the heat, then simmer for 6–8 minutes, shaking the pan occasionally, until the vegetables are just tender.

3 Season the vegetables to taste with salt and pepper, then stir in the chopped fresh parsley and snipped chives. Cook the vegetables for a few seconds more, stirring them once or twice until the herbs are well mixed, then serve at once with grilled lamb chops or roast chicken.

COOK'S TIP
You can make this dish in the winter too, but cut larger, tougher vegetables into chunks and cook for slightly longer.

NUTRITION NOTES

Per portion:

Energy	36Kcals/152kJ
Fat	0.45g
Saturated fat	0
Cholesterol	0
Fibre	2.35g

SPICY JACKET POTATOES

Serves 2–4
2 large baking potatoes
5ml/1 tsp sunflower oil
1 small onion, finely chopped
2.5cm/1in piece fresh ginger root, grated
5ml/1 tsp ground cumin
5ml/1 tsp ground coriander
2.5ml/½ tsp ground turmeric
garlic salt
natural yogurt and fresh coriander
  sprigs, to serve

1 Preheat the oven to 190°C/375°F/ Gas 5. Prick the potatoes with a fork. Bake for 40 minutes, or until soft.

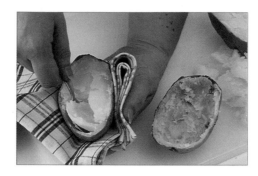

2 Cut the potatoes in half and scoop out the flesh. Heat the oil in a non-stick pan and fry the onion for a few minutes to soften. Stir in the ginger, cumin, coriander and turmeric.

3 Stir over a low heat for about 2 minutes, then add the potato flesh, and garlic salt, to taste.

4 Cook the potato mixture for a further 2 minutes, stirring occasion-ally. Spoon the mixture back into the potato shells and top each with a spoonful of natural yogurt and a sprig or two of fresh coriander. Serve hot.

NUTRITION NOTES

Per portion:
Energy	212Kcals/890kJ
Fat	2.54g
Saturated fat	0.31g
Cholesterol	0.4mg
Fibre	3.35g

TWO BEANS PROVENÇAL

Serves 4
5ml/1 tsp olive oil
1 small onion, finely chopped
1 garlic clove, crushed
225g/8oz French beans
225g/8oz runner beans
2 tomatoes, skinned and chopped
salt and black pepper

NUTRITION NOTES

Per portion:
Energy	68Kcals/286kJ
Fat	1.76g
Saturated fat	0.13g
Cholesterol	0
Fibre	5.39g

1 Heat the oil in a heavy-based, or non-stick, pan and sauté the chopped onion over a medium heat until softened but not browned.

2 Add the garlic, the French and runner beans and the tomatoes, then season well and cover tightly.

3 Cook over a fairly low heat, shaking the pan occasionally, for about 30 minutes, or until the beans are tender. Serve hot.

BROCCOLI CAULIFLOWER GRATIN

Broccoli and cauliflower make an attractive combination, and this dish is much lighter than a classic cauliflower cheese.

INGREDIENTS

Serves 4
1 small cauliflower (about 250g/9oz)
1 small head broccoli (about 250g/9oz)
150g/5oz/½ cup natural low fat yogurt
75g/3oz/1 cup grated reduced fat
  Cheddar cheese
5ml/1 tsp wholegrain mustard
30ml/2 tbsp wholemeal breadcrumbs
salt and black pepper

1 Break the cauliflower and broccoli into florets and cook in lightly salted, boiling water for 8–10 minutes, until just tender. Drain well and transfer to a flameproof dish.

2 Mix together the yogurt, grated cheese and mustard, then season the mixture with pepper and spoon over the cauliflower and broccoli.

3 Sprinkle the breadcrumbs over the top and place under a moderately hot grill until golden brown. Serve hot.

COOK'S TIP
When preparing the cauliflower and broccoli, discard the tougher part of the stalk, then break the florets into even-sized pieces, so they cook evenly.

NUTRITION NOTES

Per portion:	
Energy	144Kcals/601kJ
Fat	6.5g
Saturated fat	3.25g
Cholesterol	16.5mg
Fibre	3.25g

WATERCRESS POTATO SALAD BOWL

New potatoes are equally good hot or cold, and this colourful, nutritious salad is an ideal way of making the most of them.

INGREDIENTS

Serves 4

450g/1 lb small new potatoes, unpeeled
1 bunch watercress
200g/7oz/1½ cups cherry tomatoes, halved
30ml/2 tbsp pumpkin seeds
45ml/3 tbsp low fat fromage frais
15ml/1 tbsp cider vinegar
5ml/1 tsp soft light brown sugar
salt and paprika

1 Cook the potatoes in lightly salted, boiling water until just tender, then drain and leave to cool.

2 Toss together the potatoes, watercress, tomatoes and pumpkin seeds.

3 Place the fromage frais, vinegar, sugar, salt and paprika in a screw-topped jar and shake well to mix. Pour over the salad just before serving.

NUTRITION NOTES

Per portion:

Energy	150Kcals/630kJ
Fat	4.15g
Saturated fat	0.81g
Cholesterol	0.11mg
Fibre	2.55g

COOK'S TIP
If you are packing this salad for a picnic, take the dressing in the jar and toss in just before serving.

BEETROOT, CHICORY AND ORANGE SALAD

A refreshing salad which goes well with grilled meats or fish. Alternatively, arrange it prettily on individual plates and serve as a summer starter.

INGREDIENTS

Serves 4
2 medium cooked beetroot, diced
2 heads chicory, sliced
1 large orange
60ml/4 tbsp natural low fat yogurt
10ml/2 tsp wholegrain mustard
salt and black pepper

1 Mix together the diced cooked beetroot and sliced chicory in a large serving bowl.

2 Finely grate the rind from the orange. With a sharp knife, remove all the peel and white pith. Cut out the segments, catching the juice in a bowl. Add the segments to the salad.

3 Add the orange rind, yogurt, mustard and seasonings to the orange juice, mix thoroughly, then spoon over the salad.

> **COOK'S TIP**
> Fresh baby spinach leaves or rocket could be used in place of the chicory, if you prefer.

NUTRITION NOTES	
Per portion:	
Energy	41Kcals/172kJ
Fat	0.60g
Saturated fat	0.08g
Cholesterol	0.60mg
Fibre	1.42g

ROASTED PEPPER SALAD

This colourful salad is very easy and can be made up to a day in advance, as the sharp-sweet dressing mingles with the mild pepper flavours.

INGREDIENTS

Serves 4
3 large red, green and yellow peppers, halved and seeded
115g/4oz feta cheese, diced or crumbled
15ml/1 tbsp sherry vinegar or red wine vinegar
15ml/1 tbsp clear honey
salt and black pepper

1 Arrange the pepper halves in a single layer, skin side upwards, on a baking sheet. Place the peppers under a hot grill until the skin is blackened and beginning to blister.

2 Lift the peppers into a plastic bag and close the end. Leave until cool, then peel off and discard the skin.

3 Arrange the peppers on a platter and scatter the cheese over them. Mix together the vinegar, honey and seasonings, then sprinkle over the salad. Chill until ready to serve.

NUTRITION NOTES	
Per portion:	
Energy	110Kcals/462kJ
Fat	6.15g
Saturated fat	3.65g
Cholesterol	20.13mg
Fibre	1.84g

ROSEMARY ROASTIES

These unusual roast potatoes use far less fat than traditional roast potatoes, and because they still have their skins they not only absorb less oil but have more flavour too.

──── INGREDIENTS ────

Serves 4
1kg/2 lb small red potatoes
10ml/2 tsp walnut or sunflower oil
30ml/2 tbsp fresh rosemary leaves
salt and paprika

1 Preheat the oven to 240°C/475°F/ Gas 9. Leave the potatoes whole with the peel on, or if large, cut in half. Place the potatoes in a large pan of cold water and bring to the boil. Drain well.

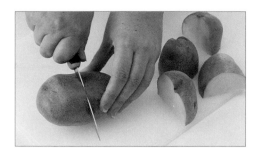

2 Drizzle the walnut or sunflower oil over the potatoes and shake the pan to coat them evenly.

3 Tip the potatoes into a shallow roasting tin. Sprinkle with rosemary, salt and paprika. Roast for 30 minutes or until crisp. Serve hot.

──── NUTRITION NOTES ────

Per portion:

Energy	205Kcals/865kJ
Fat	2.22g
Saturated fat	0.19g
Cholesterol	0
Fibre	3.25g

BAKED COURGETTES IN PASSATA

──── INGREDIENTS ────

Serves 4
5ml/1 tsp olive oil
3 large courgettes, thinly sliced
½ small red onion, finely chopped
300ml/½ pint/1¼ cups passata
30ml/2 tbsp chopped fresh thyme
garlic salt and black pepper
fresh thyme sprigs, to garnish

1 Preheat the oven to 190°C/375°F/ Gas 5. Brush an ovenproof dish with olive oil. Arrange half the courgettes and onion in the dish.

2 Spoon half the passata over the vegetables and sprinkle with some of the fresh thyme, then season to taste with garlic salt and pepper.

3 Arrange the remaining courgettes and onion in the dish on top of the passata, then season to taste with more garlic salt and pepper. Spoon over the remaining passata and spread evenly.

4 Cover the dish with foil, then bake for 40–45 minutes, or until the courgettes are tender. Garnish with sprigs of thyme and serve hot.

──── NUTRITION NOTES ────

Per portion:

Energy	49Kcals/205kJ
Fat	1.43g
Saturated fat	0.22g
Cholesterol	0
Fibre	1.73g

HOT PUDDINGS

Pudding-lovers will be glad to learn that proper puds need not be taboo for low fat diets. There are lots of ways to cook quite substantial hot puddings without the need for high-fat, rich mixtures. Classic crumbles can be made a little less sinful and far more exciting by adding less fat and more crunch in the form of oats or nuts. Skimmed or semi-skimmed milk, with a little whisked egg white, will lighten a milk pudding, and egg whites can be used in place of whole eggs for pancakes or batter puddings. For a change try an unusual couscous or breadcrumb mixture instead of a heavy sponge pudding. Even a delicious, sticky Gingerbread Upside Down Pudding can be made with just a little oil and the minimum of eggs, with no loss of pud-appeal.

BANANA, MAPLE AND LIME PANCAKES

Pancakes are a treat any day of the week, and they can be made in advance and stored in the freezer for convenience.

INGREDIENTS

Serves 4
115g/4oz/1 cup plain flour
1 egg white
250ml/8 fl oz/1 cup skimmed milk
50ml/2 fl oz/¼ cup cold water
sunflower oil, for frying

For the filling
4 bananas, sliced
45ml/3 tbsp maple syrup or golden syrup
30ml/2 tbsp lime juice
strips of lime rind, to decorate

1 Beat together the flour, egg white, milk and water until smooth and bubbly. Chill until needed.

2 Heat a small amount of oil in a non-stick frying pan and pour in enough batter just to coat the base. Swirl it around the pan to coat evenly.

3 Cook until golden, then toss or turn and cook the other side. Place on a plate, cover with foil and keep hot while making the remaining pancakes.

4 To make the filling, place the bananas, syrup and lime juice in a pan and simmer gently for 1 minute. Spoon into the pancakes and fold into quarters. Sprinkle with shreds of lime rind to decorate. Serve hot, with yogurt or low fat fromage frais.

COOK'S TIP
Pancakes freeze well. To store for later use, interleave them with non-stick baking paper, overwrap and freeze for up to 3 months.

NUTRITION NOTES	
Per portion:	
Energy	282Kcals/1185kJ
Fat	2.79g
Saturated fat	0.47g
Cholesterol	1.25mg
Fibre	2.12g

SPICED PEARS IN CIDER

Any variety of pear can be used for cooking, but it is best to choose firm pears for this recipe, or they will break up easily – Conference are a good choice.

INGREDIENTS

Serves 4

4 medium firm pears
250ml/8 fl oz/1 cup dry cider
thinly pared strip of lemon rind
1 cinnamon stick
30ml/2 tbsp light muscovado sugar
5ml/1 tsp arrowroot
ground cinnamon, to sprinkle

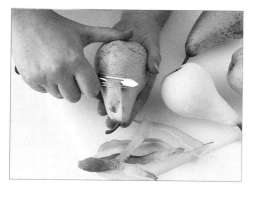

1 Peel the pears thinly, leaving them whole with the stalks on. Place in a pan with the cider, lemon rind and cinnamon. Cover and simmer gently, turning the pears occasionally for 15–20 minutes, or until tender.

2 Lift out the pears. Boil the syrup, uncovered to reduce by about half. Remove the lemon rind and cinnamon stick, then stir in the sugar.

3 Mix the arrowroot with 15ml/ 1 tbsp cold water in a small bowl until smooth, then stir into the syrup. Bring to the boil and stir over the heat until thickened and clear.

4 Pour the sauce over the pears and sprinkle with ground cinnamon. Leave to cool slightly, then serve warm with low fat fromage frais.

COOK'S TIP
Whole pears look very impressive, but if you prefer, they can be halved and cored before cooking. This will shorten the cooking time slightly.

NUTRITION NOTES
Per portion:

Energy	102Kcals/428kJ
Fat	0.18g
Saturated fat	0.01g
Cholesterol	0
Fibre	1.65g

SNOW-CAPPED APPLES

INGREDIENTS

Serves 4

4 small Bramley cooking apples
90ml/6 tbsp orange marmalade or jam
2 egg whites
50g/2oz/4 tbsp caster sugar

1 Preheat the oven to 180°C/350°F/ Gas 4. Core the apples and score through the skins around the middle with a sharp knife.

2 Place in a wide ovenproof dish and spoon 15ml/1 tbsp marmalade into the centre of each. Cover and bake for 35–40 minutes, or until tender.

3 Whisk the egg whites in a large bowl until stiff enough to hold soft peaks. Whisk in the sugar, then fold in the remaining marmalade.

4 Spoon the meringue over the apples, then return to the oven for 10–15 minutes, or until golden. Serve hot.

NUTRITION NOTES

Per portion:

Energy	165Kcals/394kJ
Fat	0.16g
Saturated fat	0
Cholesterol	0
Fibre	1.9g

STRAWBERRY APPLE TART

INGREDIENTS

Serves 4–6

150g/5oz/1¼ cups self-raising flour
50g/2oz/⅔ cup rolled oats
50g/2oz/4 tbsp sunflower margarine
2 medium Bramley cooking apples,
   about 450g/1 lb total weight
200g/7oz/2 cups strawberries, halved
50g/2oz/4 tbsp caster sugar
15ml/1 tbsp cornflour

1 Preheat the oven to 200°C/400°F/ Gas 6. Mix together the flour and oats in a large bowl and rub in the margarine evenly. Stir in just enough cold water to bind the mixture to a firm dough. Knead lightly until smooth.

2 Roll out the pastry and line a 23cm/9in loose-based flan tin. Trim the edges, prick the base and line with greaseproof paper and baking beans. Roll out the pastry trimmings and stamp out heart shapes using a cutter.

3 Bake the pastry case for 10 minutes, remove paper and beans and bake for 10–15 minutes or until golden brown. Bake the hearts until golden.

4 Peel, core and slice the apples. Place in a pan with the strawberries, sugar and cornflour. Cover and cook gently, stirring, until the fruit is just tender. Spoon into the pastry case and decorate with pastry hearts.

NUTRITION NOTES

Per portion:

Energy	382Kcals/1602kJ
Fat	11.93g
Saturated fat	2.18g
Cholesterol	0.88mg
Fibre	4.37g

FRUITY BREAD PUDDING

A delicious family favourite pud from grandmother's day, with a lighter, healthier touch.

INGREDIENTS

Serves 4

75g/3oz/⅔ cup mixed dried fruit
150ml/¼ pint/⅔ cup apple juice
115g/4oz stale brown or white bread, diced
5ml/1 tsp mixed spice
1 large banana, sliced
150ml/¼ pint/⅔ cup skimmed milk
15ml/1 tbsp demerara sugar
natural low fat yogurt, to serve

1 Preheat the oven to 200°C/400°F/ Gas 6. Place the dried fruit in a small pan with the apple juice and bring to the boil.

2 Remove the pan from the heat and stir in the bread, spice and banana Spoon the mixture into a shallow 1.2 litre/2 pint/5 cup ovenproof dish and pour over the milk.

3 Sprinkle with demerara sugar and bake for 25–30 minutes, until firm and golden brown. Serve hot or cold with natural yogurt.

COOK'S TIP
Different types of bread will absorb varying amounts of liquid, so you may need to adjust the amount of milk to allow for this.

NUTRITION NOTES

Per portion:

Energy	190Kcals/800kJ
Fat	0.89g
Saturated fat	0.21g
Cholesterol	0.75mg
Fibre	1.8g

SOUFFLÉED ORANGE SEMOLINA

Semolina has a poor reputation as a rather dull, sloppy pudding, but cooked like this you would hardly recognise it.

INGREDIENTS

Serves 4

50g/2oz/¼ cup semolina
600ml/1 pint/2½ cups semi-skimmed milk
30ml/2 tbsp light muscovado sugar
1 large orange
1 egg white

1 Preheat the oven to 200°C/400°F/ Gas 6. Place the semolina in a non-stick pan with the milk and sugar. Stir over a moderate heat until thickened and smooth. Remove from the heat.

2 Grate a few long shreds of orange rind from the orange and save for decoration. Finely grate the remaining rind. Cut all the peel and white pith from the orange and remove the segments. Stir into the semolina with the orange rind.

3 Whisk the egg white until stiff but not dry, then fold lightly and evenly into the mixture. Spoon into a 1 litre/ 1¾ pint/4 cup ovenproof dish and bake for 15–20 minutes, until risen and golden brown. Serve immediately.

COOK'S TIP
When using the rind of citrus fruit, scrub the fruit thoroughly before use, or buy unwaxed fruit.

NUTRITION NOTES

Per portion:

Energy	158Kcals/665kJ
Fat	2.67g
Saturated fat	1.54g
Cholesterol	10.5mg
Fibre	0.86g

SPICED RED FRUIT COMPOTE

INGREDIENTS

Serves 4

4 ripe red plums, halved
225g/8oz/2 cups strawberries, halved
225g/8oz/1¾ cups raspberries
30ml/2 tbsp light muscovado sugar
30 ml/2 tbsp cold water
1 cinnamon stick
3 pieces star anise
6 cloves

NUTRITION NOTES

Per portion:

Energy	90Kcals/375kJ
Fat	0.32g
Saturated fat	0
Cholesterol	0
Fibre	3.38g

1 Place the plums, strawberries and raspberies in a heavy-based pan with the sugar and water.

2 Add the cinnamon stick, star anise and cloves to the pan and heat gently, without boiling, until the sugar dissolves and the fruit juices run.

3 Cover the pan and leave the fruit to infuse over a very low heat for about 5 minutes. Remove the spices from the compote before serving warm with natural yogurt or fromage frais.

RHUBARB SPIRAL COBBLER

INGREDIENTS

Serves 4

675g/1½ lb rhubarb, sliced
50g/2oz/4 tbsp caster sugar
45ml/3 tbsp orange juice
200g/7oz/1⅓ cups self-raising flour
30ml/2 tbsp caster sugar
about 200g/7oz/1 cup natural yogurt
grated rind of 1 medium orange
30ml/2 tbsp demerara sugar
5ml/1 tsp ground ginger

1 Preheat the oven to 200°C/400°F/ Gas 6. Cook the rhubarb, sugar and orange juice in a covered pan until tender. Tip into an ovenproof dish.

2 To make the topping, mix the flour and caster sugar, then stir enough of the yogurt to bind to a soft dough.

3 Roll out on a floured surface to a 25cm/10in square. Mix the orange rind, demerara sugar and ginger, then sprinkle this over the dough.

4 Roll up quite tightly, then cut into about 10 slices using a sharp knife. Arrange the slices over the rhubarb.

5 Bake in the oven for 15–20 minutes, or until the spirals are well risen and golden brown. Serve warm, with yogurt or custard.

NUTRITION NOTES

Per portion:

Energy	320Kcals/1343kJ
Fat	1.2g
Saturated fat	0.34g
Cholesterol	2mg
Fibre	3.92g

CRUNCHY GOOSEBERRY CRUMBLE

Gooseberries are perfect for traditional family puddings like this one. When they are out of season, other fruits such as apple, plums or rhubarb could be used instead.

INGREDIENTS

Serves 4
500g/1¼ lb/5 cups gooseberries
50g/2oz/4 tbsp caster sugar
75g/3oz/1 cup rolled oats
75g/3oz/¾ cup wholemeal flour
60ml/4 tbsp sunflower oil
50g/2oz/4 tbsp demerara sugar
30ml/2 tbsp chopped walnuts
natural yogurt or custard, to serve

1 Preheat the oven to 200°C/400°F/ Gas 6. Place the gooseberries in a pan with the caster sugar. Cover the pan and cook over a low heat for 10 minutes, until the gooseberries are just tender. Tip into an ovenproof dish.

2 To make the crumble, place the oats, flour and oil in a bowl and stir with a fork until evenly mixed.

3 Stir in the demerara sugar and walnuts, then spread evenly over the gooseberries. Bake for 25–30 minutes, or until golden and bubbling. Serve hot with yogurt, or custard made with skimmed milk.

COOK'S TIP
The best cooking gooseberries are the early small, firm green ones.

NUTRITION NOTES

Per portion:
Energy	422Kcals/1770kJ
Fat	18.5g
Saturated fat	2.32g
Cholesterol	0
Fibre	5.12g

GINGERBREAD UPSIDE DOWN PUDDING

A proper pudding goes down well on a cold winter's day. This one is quite quick to make and looks very impressive.

INGREDIENTS

Serves 4 – 6
sunflower oil, for brushing
15ml/1 tbsp soft brown sugar
4 medium peaches, halved and stoned,
*   or canned peach halves*
8 walnut halves

For the base
130g/4½oz/½ cup wholemeal flour
2.5ml/½ tsp bicarbonate of soda
7.5ml/1½ tsp ground ginger
5ml/1 tsp ground cinnamon
115g/4oz/½ cup molasses sugar
1 egg
120ml/4 fl oz/½ cup skimmed milk
50ml/2 fl oz/¼ cup sunflower oil

1 Preheat the oven to 175°C/350°F/ Gas 4. For the topping, brush the base and sides of a 23cm/9in round springform cake tin with oil. Sprinkle the sugar over the base.

2 Arrange the peaches cut-side down in the tin with a walnut half in each.

3 For the base, sift together the flour, bicarbonate of soda, ginger and cinnamon, then stir in the sugar. Beat together the egg, milk and oil, then mix into the dry ingredients until smooth.

4 Pour the mixture evenly over the peaches and bake for 35–40 minutes, until firm to the touch. Turn out onto a serving plate. Serve hot with yogurt or custard.

NUTRITION NOTES

Per portion:	
Energy	432Kcals/1812kJ
Fat	16.54g
Saturated fat	2.27g
Cholesterol	48.72mg
Fibre	4.79g

Hot Plum Batter

Other fruits can be used in place of plums, depending on the season. Canned black cherries are also a convenient storecupboard substitute.

INGREDIENTS

Serves 4
450g/1 lb ripe red plums, quartered and stoned
200ml/7 fl oz/⅞ cup skimmed milk
60ml/4 tbsp skimmed milk powder
15ml/1 tbsp light muscovado sugar
5ml/1 tsp vanilla essence
75g/3oz self-raising flour
2 egg whites
icing sugar, to sprinkle

1 Preheat the oven to 220°C/425°F/ Gas 7. Lightly oil a wide, shallow ovenproof dish and add the plums.

2 Pour the milk, milk powder, sugar, vanilla, flour and egg whites into a food processor. Process until smooth.

3 Pour the batter over the plums. Bake for 25–30 minutes, or until well risen and golden. Sprinkle with icing sugar and serve immediately.

NUTRITION NOTES	
Per portion:	
Energy	195Kcals/816kJ
Fat	0.48g
Saturated fat	0.12g
Cholesterol	2.8mg
Fibre	2.27g

Glazed Apricot Sponge

Proper puddings are usually very high in saturated fat, but this one uses the minimum of oil and no eggs.

INGREDIENTS

Serves 4
10ml/2 tsp golden syrup
411g/14½oz can apricot halves in fruit juice
150g/5oz/1¼ cup self-raising flour
75g/3oz/1½ cups fresh breadcrumbs
90g/3½oz/⅔ cup light muscovado sugar
5ml/1 tsp ground cinnamon
30ml/2 tbsp sunflower oil
175ml/6 fl oz/¾ cup skimmed milk

1 Preheat the oven to 180°C/350°F/ Gas 4. Lightly oil a 900ml/1½ pint/3¾ cup pudding basin. Spoon in the syrup.

2 Drain the apricots and reserve the juice. Arrange about 8 halves in the basin. Purée the rest of the apricots with the juice and set aside.

3 Mix the flour, breadcrumbs, sugar and cinnamon then beat in the oil and milk. Spoon into the basin and bake for 50–55 minutes, or until firm and golden. Turn out and serve with the puréed fruit as a sauce.

NUTRITION NOTES	
Per portion:	
Energy	364Kcals/1530kJ
Fat	6.47g
Saturated fat	0.89g
Cholesterol	0.88mg
Fibre	2.37g

PLUM FILO POCKETS

INGREDIENTS

Serves 4

115g/4oz/½ cup skimmed milk soft
  cheese
15ml/1 tbsp light muscovado sugar
2.5ml/½ tsp ground cloves
8 large, firm plums, halved and stoned
8 sheets filo pastry
sunflower oil, for brushing
icing sugar, to sprinkle

1 Preheat the oven to 220°C/425°F/
Gas 7. Mix together the cheese,
sugar and cloves.

2 Sandwich the plum halves back
together in twos with a spoonful of
the cheese mixture.

3 Spread out the pastry and cut into
16 pieces, about 23cm/9in square.
Brush one lightly with oil and place a
second at a diagonal on top. Repeat
with the remaining squares.

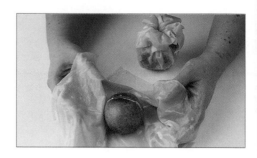

4 Place a plum on each pastry square,
and pinch corners together. Place on
baking sheet. Bake for 15–18 minutes,
until golden, then dust with icing sugar.

NUTRITION NOTES

Per portion:

Energy	188Kcals/790kJ
Fat	1.87g
Saturated fat	0.27g
Cholesterol	0.29mg
Fibre	2.55g

APPLE COUSCOUS PUDDING

This unusual mixture makes a
delicious family pudding with a
rich fruity flavour, but virtually
no fat.

INGREDIENTS

Serves 4

600ml/1 pint/2½ cups apple juice
115g/4oz/⅔ cup couscous
40g/1½ oz/¼ cup sultanas
2.5ml/½ tsp mixed spice
1 large Bramley cooking apple, peeled,
  cored and sliced
30ml/2 tbsp demerara sugar
natural low fat yogurt, to serve

1 Preheat the oven to 200°C/400°F/
Gas 6. Place the apple juice, couscous, sultanas and spice in a pan and
bring to the boil, stirring. Cover and
simmer for 10–12 minutes, until all the
free liquid is absorbed.

2 Spoon half the couscous mixture
into a 1.2 litre/2 pint/5 cup ovenproof dish and top with half the apple
slices. Top with remaining couscous.

3 Arrange the remaining apple slices
overlapping over the top and sprinkle with demerara sugar. Bake for
25–30 minutes or until golden brown.
Serve hot, with yogurt.

NUTRITION NOTES

Per portion:

Energy	194Kcals/815kJ
Fat	0.58g
Saturated fat	0.09g
Cholesterol	0
Fibre	0.75g

COLD DESSERTS

From fresh, colourful fruit salads to refreshing, tangy sorbets, healthy cold desserts should be the easiest part of selecting dishes for your low fat menus. The year-round huge variety of fresh fruit gives a head start – even the simplest platter of fresh fruits can make an exotic dessert. Time was when ice creams, mousses and cheesecakes were without exception rich, elaborate and high fat, certainly to be avoided in excess. But the rapidly expanding range of low fat dairy products such as fromage frais, yogurts, and crème fraîche, means that lighter, far less rich versions are now possible. So, if plain fresh fruit is just not enough, you can tuck into a luscious scoop of Banana Honey Yogurt Ice or a slice of Creamy Mango Cheesecake with not a trace of guilt.

FRUITED RICE RING

This unusual rice pudding looks beautiful turned out of a ring mould but if you prefer, stir the fruit into the rice and serve in individual dishes.

INGREDIENTS

Serves 4

65g/2½oz/5 tbsp short grain rice
900ml/1½ pint/3¾ cups semi-skimmed milk
1 cinnamon stick
175g/6oz/1½ cups dried fruit salad
175ml/6 fl oz/¾ cup orange juice
45ml/3 tbsp caster sugar
finely grated rind of 1 small orange

1 Place the rice, milk and cinnamon stick in a large pan and bring to the boil. Cover and simmer, stirring occasionally, for about 1½ hours, until no free liquid remains.

2 Meanwhile, place the fruit and orange juice in a pan and bring to the boil. Cover and simmer very gently for about 1 hour, until tender and no free liquid remains.

3 Remove the cinnamon stick from the rice and stir in the sugar and orange rind.

4 Tip the fruit into the base of a lightly oiled 1.5 litre/2½ pint/6 cup ring mould. Spoon the rice over, smoothing down firmly. Chill.

5 Run a knife around the edge of the mould and turn out the rice carefully on to a serving plate.

NUTRITION NOTES	
Per portion:	
Energy	343Kcals/1440kJ
Fat	4.4g
Saturated fat	2.26g
Cholesterol	15.75mg
Fibre	1.07g

RASPBERRY PASSION FRUIT SWIRLS

If passion fruit is not available, this simple dessert can be made with raspberries alone.

INGREDIENTS

Serves 4

300g/11oz/2½ cups raspberries
2 passion fruit
*400g/14oz/1⅔ cups low fat fromage
    frais*
30ml/2 tbsp caster sugar
*raspberries and sprigs of mint, to
    decorate*

1 Mash the raspberries in a small bowl with a fork until the juice runs. Scoop out the passion fruit pulp into a separate bowl with the fromage frais and sugar and mix well.

2 Spoon alternate spoonfuls of the raspberry pulp and the fromage frais mixture into stemmed glasses or one large serving dish, stirring lightly to create a swirled effect.

3 Decorate each dessert with a whole raspberry and a sprig of fresh mint. Serve chilled.

COOK'S TIP
Over-ripe, slightly soft fruit can also be used in this recipe. Use frozen raspberries when fresh are not available, but thaw first.

NUTRITION NOTES

Per portion:

Energy	110Kcals/462kJ
Fat	0.47g
Saturated fat	0.13g
Cholesterol	1mg
Fibre	2.12g

CREAMY MANGO CHEESECAKE

Cheesecakes are always a favourite but sadly they are often high in fat. This one is the exception.

INGREDIENTS

Serves 4

115g/4oz/1¼ cups rolled oats
40g/1½oz/3 tbsp sunflower margarine
30ml/2 tbsp clear honey
1 large ripe mango
300g/10oz/1¼ cups low fat soft cheese
150g/5oz/⅔ cup low fat natural
   yogurt
finely grated rind of 1 small lime
45ml/3 tbsp apple juice
20ml/4 tsp powdered gelatine
fresh mango and lime slices, to decorate

1 Preheat the oven to 200°C/400°F/ Gas 6. Mix together the oats, margarine and honey. Press the mixture into the base of a 20cm/8in loose-bottomed cake tin. Bake for 12–15 minutes, until lightly browned. Cool.

2 Peel, stone and roughly chop the mango. Place the chopped mango, cheese, yogurt and lime rind in a food processor and process until smooth.

3 Heat the apple juice until boiling, sprinkle the gelatine over it, stir to dissolve, then stir into cheese mixture.

4 Pour the cheese mixture into the tin and chill until set, then turn out on to a serving plate. Decorate the top with mango and lime slices.

NUTRITION NOTES

Per portion:

Energy	422Kcals/1774kJ
Fat	11.37g
Saturated fat	2.2g
Cholesterol	2.95mg
Fibre	7.15g

FRUDITÉS WITH HONEY DIP

INGREDIENTS

Serves 4

225g/8oz/1 cup Greek-style yogurt
45ml/3 tbsp clear honey
selection of fresh fruit for dipping such
   as apples, pears, tangerines, grapes,
   figs, cherries, strawberries and kiwi
   fruit

NUTRITION NOTES

Per portion:

Energy	161Kcals/678kJ
Fat	5.43g
Saturated fat	3.21g
Cholesterol	7.31mg
Fibre	2.48g

1 Place the yogurt in a dish, beat until smooth, then stir in the honey, leaving a little marbled effect.

2 Cut the fruits into wedges or bite-sized pieces or leave whole.

3 Arrange the fruits on a platter with the bowl of dip in the centre. Serve chilled.

APRICOT MOUSSE

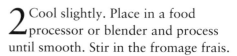

This light, fluffy dessert can be made with any dried fruits instead of apricots – try dried peaches, prunes or apples.

INGREDIENTS

Serves 4

300g/10oz/1½ cups ready-to-eat dried apricots
300ml/½ pint/1¼ cups fresh orange juice
200g/7oz/⅞ cup low fat fromage frais
2 egg whites
mint sprigs, to decorate

1 Place the apricots in a saucepan with the orange juice and heat gently until boiling. Cover and simmer gently for 3 minutes.

2 Cool slightly. Place in a food processor or blender and process until smooth. Stir in the fromage frais.

3 Whisk the egg whites until stiff enough to hold soft peaks, then fold into the apricot mixture.

4 Spoon into four stemmed glasses or one large serving dish. Chill before serving.

COOK'S TIP
To make a speedier fool-type dish, omit the egg whites and simply swirl together the apricot mixture and fromage frais.

NUTRITION NOTES

Per portion:

Energy	180Kcals/757kJ
Fat	0.63g
Saturated fat	0.06g
Cholesterol	0.5mg
Fibre	4.8g

APPLE FOAM WITH BLACKBERRIES

Any seasonal soft fruit can be used for this if blackberries are not available.

INGREDIENTS

Serves 4

225g/8oz blackberries
150ml/¼ pint/⅔ cup apple juice
5ml/1 tsp powdered gelatine
15ml/1 tbsp clear honey
2 egg whites

1 Place the blackberries in a pan with 60ml/4 tbsp of the apple juice and heat gently until the fruit is soft. Remove from the heat, cool and chill.

2 Sprinkle the gelatine over the remaining apple juice in a small pan and stir over a low heat until dissolved. Stir in the honey.

3 Whisk the egg whites until they hold stiff peaks. Continue whisking hard and pour in the hot gelatine mixture gradually, until well mixed.

4 Quickly spoon the foam into rough mounds on individual plates. Chill. Serve with the blackberries and juice spooned around.

COOK'S TIP
Make sure that you dissolve the gelatine over a very low heat. It must not boil, or it will lose its setting ability.

NUTRITION NOTES

Per portion:

Energy	49Kcals/206kJ
Fat	0.15g
Saturated fat	0
Cholesterol	0
Fibre	1.74g

GRAPE CHEESE WHIP

INGREDIENTS

Serves 4

*150g/5oz/1 cup black or green seed-
    less grapes, plus 4 sprigs*
2 egg whites
15ml/1 tbsp caster sugar
finely grated rind and juice of ½ lemon
*225g/8oz/1 cup skimmed milk soft
    cheese*
45ml/3 tbsp clear honey
30ml/2 tbsp brandy (optional)

NUTRITION NOTES

Per portion:

Energy	135Kcals/563kJ
Fat	0
Saturated fat	0
Cholesterol	0.56mg
Fibre	0

1 Brush the sprigs of grapes lightly with egg white and sprinkle with sugar to coat. Leave to dry.

2 Mix together the lemon rind and juice, cheese, honey and brandy. Chop the remaining grapes and stir in.

3 Whisk the egg whites until stiff enough to hold soft peaks. Fold the whites into the grape mixture, then spoon into serving glasses.

4 Top with sugar-frosted grapes and serve chilled.

STRAWBERRIES IN SPICED GRAPE JELLY

INGREDIENTS

Serves 4

450ml/¾ pint/1⅞cups red grape juice
1 cinnamon stick
1 small orange
15ml/1 tbsp/1 envelope gelatine
225g/8oz strawberries, chopped
*strawberries and orange rind, to
    decorate*

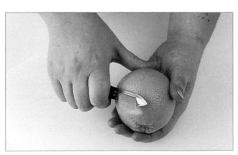

1 Place the grape juice in a pan with the cinnamon. Thinly pare the rind from the orange and add to the pan. Infuse over a very low heat for 10 minutes, then remove the flavourings.

2 Squeeze the juice from the orange and sprinkle over the gelatine. Stir into the grape juice to dissolve. Allow to cool until just beginning to set.

3 Stir in the strawberries and quickly tip into a 1 litre/1¾pint/4 cup mould or serving dish. Chill until set.

4 To turn out, dip the mould quickly into hot water and invert on to a serving plate. Decorate with fresh strawberries and shreds of orange rind.

NUTRITION NOTES

Per portion:

Energy	85Kcals/355kJ
Fat	0.2g
Saturated fat	0
Cholesterol	0
Fibre	1.04g

PLUM AND PORT SORBET

Rather a grown-up sorbet, this one, but you could use fresh, still red grape juice in place of the port if you prefer.

INGREDIENTS

Serves 4–6
*1kg/2 lb ripe red plums, halved and
  stoned*
75g/3oz/6 tbsp caster sugar
45ml/3 tbsp water
45ml/3 tbsp ruby port or red wine
crisp, sweet biscuits, to serve

1 Place the plums in a pan with the sugar and water. Stir over a gentle heat until the sugar is melted, then cover and simmer gently for about 5 minutes, until the fruit is soft.

2 Turn into a food processor and purée until smooth, then stir in the port. Cool completely, then tip into a freezer container and freeze until firm around the edges.

3 Spoon into the food processor and process until smooth. Return to the freezer and freeze until solid.

4 Allow to soften slightly at room temperature for 15–20 minutes before serving in scoops, with sweet biscuits.

NUTRITION NOTES	
Per portion:	
Energy	166Kcals/699kJ
Fat	0.25g
Saturated fat	0
Cholesterol	0
Fibre	3.75g

TOFU BERRY BRULÉE

This is a lighter variation of a classic dessert, usually forbidden on a low fat diet, using tofu, which is low in fat and free from cholesterol. Use any soft fruits in season.

INGREDIENTS

Serves 4
300g/11oz packet silken tofu
45ml/3 tbsp icing sugar
225g/8oz/1½ cups red berry fruits,
*   such as raspberries, strawberries and*
*   redcurrants*
about 75ml/5 tbsp demerara sugar

1 Place the tofu and icing sugar in a food processor or blender and process until smooth.

2 Stir in the fruits and spoon into a 900ml/1½ pint/3¾ cup flameproof dish. Sprinkle the top with enough demerara sugar to cover evenly.

3 Place under a very hot grill until the sugar melts and caramelises. Chill before serving.

COOK'S TIP
Choose silken tofu rather than firm tofu as it gives a smoother texture in this type of dish. Firm tofu is better for cooking in chunks.

NUTRITION NOTES

Per portion:

Energy	180Kcals/760kJ
Fat	3.01g
Saturated fat	0.41g
Cholesterol	0
Fibre	1.31g

EMERALD FRUIT SALAD

INGREDIENTS

Serves 4

30ml/2 tbsp lime juice
30ml/2 tbsp clear honey
2 green eating apples, cored and sliced
1 small ripe Ogen melon, diced
2 kiwi fruit, sliced
1 star fruit, sliced
mint sprigs, to decorate

1 Mix together the lime juice and honey in a large bowl, then toss the apple slices in this.

2 Stir in the melon, kiwi fruit and star fruit. Place in a glass serving dish and chill before serving.

3 Decorate with mint sprigs and serve with yogurt or fromage frais.

COOK'S TIP
Starfruit is best when fully ripe – look for plump, yellow fruit.

NUTRITION NOTES

Per portion:

Energy	93Kcals/390kJ
Fat	0.48g
Saturated fat	0
Cholesterol	0
Fibre	2.86g

PEACH AND GINGER PASHKA

This simpler adaptation of a Russian Easter favourite is made with much lighter ingredients than the traditional version.

INGREDIENTS

Serves 4–6

350g/12oz/1½ cups low fat cottage cheese
2 ripe peaches or nectarines
90g/3½oz/⅓ cup low fat natural yogurt
2 pieces stem ginger in syrup, drained and chopped
30ml/2 tbsp stem ginger syrup
2.5ml/½ tsp vanilla essence
peach slices and toasted flaked almonds, to decorate

NUTRITION NOTES

Per portion:

Energy	142Kcals/600kJ
Fat	1.63g
Saturated fat	0.22g
Cholesterol	1.77mg
Fibre	1.06g

1 Drain the cottage cheese and rub through a sieve into a bowl. Stone and roughly chop the peaches.

2 Mix together the chopped peaches, cottage cheese, yogurt, ginger, syrup and vanilla essence.

3 Line a new, clean flowerpot or a sieve with a piece of clean, fine cloth such as muslin.

4 Tip in the cheese mixture, then wrap over the cloth and place a weight on top. Leave over a bowl in a cool place to drain overnight. To serve, unwrap the cloth and invert the pashka on to a plate. Decorate with peach slices and almonds.

BANANA HONEY YOGURT ICE

INGREDIENTS

Serves 4–6

4 ripe bananas, chopped roughly
15ml/1 tbsp lemon juice
30ml/2 tbsp clear honey
250g/9oz/1 cup Greek-style yogurt
2.5ml/½ tsp ground cinnamon
crisp biscuits, flaked hazelnuts and
  banana slices, to serve

NUTRITION NOTES

Per portion:

Energy	138Kcals/580kJ
Fat	7.37g
Saturated fat	3.72g
Cholesterol	8.13mg
Fibre	0.47g

1 Place the bananas in a food processor or blender with the lemon juice, honey, yogurt and cinnamon. Process until smooth and creamy.

2 Pour the mixture into a freezer container and freeze until almost solid. Spoon back into the food processor and process again until smooth.

3 Return to the freezer until firm. Allow to soften at room temperature for 15 minutes, then serve in scoops, with crisp biscuits, flaked hazelnuts and banana slices.

AUTUMN PUDDING

INGREDIENTS

Serves 6

10 slices white or brown bread, at least
  1 day old
1 Bramley cooking apple, peeled, cored
  and sliced
225g/8oz ripe red plums, halved and
  stoned
225g/8oz blackberries
60ml/4 tbsp water
75g/3oz/6 tbsp caster sugar

1 Remove the crusts from the bread and use a biscuit cutter to stamp out a 7.5cm/3in round from one slice. Cut the remaining slices in half.

2 Place the bread round in the base of a 1.2 litre/2 pint/5 cup pudding basin, then overlap the fingers around the sides, saving some for the top.

3 Place the apple, plums, blackberries, water and sugar in a pan, heat gently until the sugar dissolves, then simmer gently for 10 minutes, or until soft. Remove from the heat.

4 Reserve the juice and spoon the fruit into the bread-lined basin. Top with the reserved bread, then spoon over the reserved fruit juices.

5 Cover the mould with a saucer and place weights on top. Chill the pudding overnight. Turn out on to a serving plate and serve with low fat yogurt or fromage frais.

NUTRITION NOTES

Per portion:

Energy	197Kcals/830kJ
Fat	1.1g
Saturated fat	0.2g
Cholesterol	0
Fibre	2.84g

CAKES AND BAKES

The main advantage of baking your own cakes and biscuits is that you can control exactly what goes into them. Most commercially produced cakes and bakes contain a high proportion of saturated fats, but it is possible to bake at home using less fat, different types of fat and often less sugar too. All the bakes in this chapter are low in fat, and in many cases contain little or no eggs, and often sugar is reduced by using fruits to sweeten the mixture. The main drawback of this is that the cakes will not keep for nearly so long as traditional recipes, but it is a problem far outweighed by the health advantages. So, as you fill the biscuit tin with Apricot Yogurt Cookies or serve up that luscious slice of Carrot Cake, your conscience is clear – let them eat cake!

EGGLESS CHRISTMAS CAKE

INGREDIENTS

Makes 1 x 18cm / 7in square cake
75g/3oz/⅔ cup sultanas
75g/3oz/⅔ cup raisins
75g/3oz/½ cup currants
75g/3oz/⅓ cup glacé cherries, halved
50g/2oz/¼ cup cut mixed peel
250ml/8 fl oz/1 cup apple juice
25g/1oz/¼ cup toasted hazelnuts
30ml/2 tbsp pumpkin seeds
2 pieces stem ginger in syrup, chopped
finely grated rind of 1 lemon
120ml/4 fl oz/½ cup skimmed milk
50ml/2 fl oz/¼ cup sunflower oil
225g/8oz/1¼ cups wholemeal self-
* raising flour*
10ml/2 tsp mixed spice
45ml/3 tbsp brandy or dark rum
apricot jam, for brushing
glacé fruits, to decorate

1 Place the sultanas, raisins, currants, cherries and peel in a bowl and stir in the apple juice. Cover and leave to soak overnight.

2 Preheat the oven to 150°C/300°F/ Gas 2. Grease and line an 18cm/7in square cake tin.

3 Add the hazelnuts, pumpkin seeds, ginger and lemon rind to the soaked fruit. Stir in the milk and oil. Sift the flour and spice and stir into the mixture with the brandy or rum.

4 Spoon into the prepared tin and bake for about 1½ hours, or until the cake is golden brown and firm to the touch.

5 Turn out and cool on a wire rack. Brush with sieved apricot jam and decorate with glacé fruits.

NUTRITION NOTES

Per cake:
Energy	2702Kcals/11352kJ
Fat	73.61g
Saturated fat	10.69g
Cholesterol	2.4mg
Fibre	29.46g

CRANBERRY AND APPLE RING

Tangy cranberries add an unusual flavour to this low fat cake. It is best eaten very fresh.

INGREDIENTS

Makes 1 ring cake

225g/8oz/2 cups self-raising flour
5ml/1 tsp ground cinnamon
75g/3oz/½ cup light muscovado sugar
1 crisp eating apple, cored and diced
75g/3oz/⅔ cup fresh or frozen
  cranberries
60ml/4 tbsp sunflower oil
150ml/¼ pint/⅔ cup apple juice
cranberry jelly and apple slices, to
  decorate

1 Preheat the oven to 180°C/350°F/ Gas 4. Lightly grease a 1 litre/1¾ pint/4 cup ring tin with oil.

2 Sift together the flour and ground cinnamon, then stir in the sugar.

3 Toss together the diced apple and cranberries. Stir into the dry ingredients, then add the oil and apple juice and beat well.

4 Spoon the mixture into the prepared ring tin and bake for about 35–40 minutes, or until the cake is firm to the touch. Turn out and leave to cool completely on a wire rack.

5 To serve, drizzle warmed cranberry jelly over the cake and decorate with apple slices.

COOK'S TIP
Fresh cranberries are available throughout the winter months and if you don't use them all at once, they can be frozen for up to a year.

NUTRITION NOTES

Per cake:
Energy	1616Kcals/6787kJ
Fat	47.34g
Saturated fat	6.14g
Cholesterol	0
Fibre	12.46g

CARROT CAKE WITH LEMON FROSTING

INGREDIENTS

Makes one 18cm/7in cake

225g/8oz/1¼ cups wholemeal self-
raising flour
10ml/2 tsp ground allspice
115g/4oz/⅔ cup light muscovado
sugar
3 medium carrots (about 225g/8oz),
grated
50g/2oz/⅓ cup sultanas
75ml/5 tbsp sunflower oil
75ml/5 tbsp orange juice
75ml/5 tbsp skimmed milk
2 egg whites

For the frosting
175g/6oz/¼ cup skimmed milk soft
cheese
finely grated rind of ½ lemon
30ml/2 tbsp clear honey
shreds of lemon rind, to decorate

1 Preheat the oven to 180°C/350°F/
Gas 4. Grease a deep 18 cm/7in
round cake tin and line the base with
non-stick baking paper.

2 Sift the flour and spice, then stir in
the sugar, grated carrots and
sultanas. Mix the oil, orange juice and
milk, then stir evenly into the dry
ingredients. Whisk the egg whites until
stiff, then fold in lightly and evenly.

3 Spoon into the tin and bake for
45–50 minutes, until firm and golden.
Turn out and cool on a wire rack.

4 For the frosting, beat together the
cheese, lemon rind and honey until
smooth. Spread over the top of the
cooled cake, swirling with a palette
knife. Decorate the top with shreds of
lemon rind.

NUTRITION NOTES	
Per cake:	
Energy	2182Kcals/9167kJ
Fat	61.79g
Saturated fat	8.37g
Cholesterol	3.25mg
Fibre	26.65g

CHEWY FRUIT MUESLI SLICE

INGREDIENTS

Makes 8 slices

75g/3oz/½ cup ready-to-eat dried
apricots, chopped
1 eating apple, cored and grated
150g/5oz/1¼ cups Swiss-style muesli
150ml/¼ pint/⅔ cup apple juice
15g/½ oz/1 tbsp soft sunflower
margarine

1 Preheat the oven to 190°C/375°F/
Gas 5. Place all the ingredients in a
large bowl and mix well.

2 Press the mixture into a 20cm/8in
round, non-stick sandwich tin and
bake for 35–40 minutes, or until lightly
browned and firm.

3 Mark the muesli slice into wedges
and leave to cool in the tin.

NUTRITION NOTES	
Per portion::	
Energy	112Kcals/467kJ
Fat	2.75g
Saturated fat	0.48g
Cholesterol	0.13mg
Fibre	2.09g

BANANA ORANGE LOAF

For the best banana flavour and a really good, moist texture, make sure the bananas are very ripe for this cake.

INGREDIENTS

Makes 1 loaf
90g/3½oz/¾ cup wholemeal plain flour
90g/3½oz/¾ cup plain flour
5ml/1 tsp baking powder
5ml/1 tsp ground mixed spice
45ml/3 tbsp flaked hazelnuts, toasted
2 large ripe bananas
1 egg
30ml/2 tbsp sunflower oil
30ml/2 tbsp clear honey
finely grated rind and juice 1 small orange
4 orange slices, halved
10ml/2 tsp icing sugar

1 Preheat the oven to 180°C/350°F/ Gas 4. Brush a 1 litre/1¼ pint/4 cup loaf tin with sunflower oil and line the base with non-stick baking paper.

2 Sift the flour with the baking powder and spice into a large bowl, adding any bran that is caught in the sieve. Stir the hazelnuts into the dry ingredients.

3 Peel and mash the bananas. Beat in the egg, oil, honey and the orange rind and juice. Stir evenly into the dry ingredients.

4 Spoon into the prepared tin and smooth the top. Bake for 40–45 minutes, or until firm and golden brown. Turn out and cool on a wire rack to cool.

5 Sprinkle the orange slices with the icing sugar and grill until golden. Use to decorate the cake.

COOK'S TIP
If you plan to keep the loaf for more than two or three days, omit the orange slices, brush with honey and sprinkle with flaked hazelnuts.

NUTRITION NOTES

Per cake:

Energy	1741Kcals/7314kJ
Fat	60.74g
Saturated fat	7.39g
Cholesterol	192.5mg
Fibre	19.72g

APRICOT YOGURT COOKIES

These soft cookies are very quick to make and are useful for the biscuit tin or for lunch boxes.

─────── INGREDIENTS ───────

Makes 16
175g/6oz/1½ cups plain flour
5ml/1 tsp baking powder
5ml/1 tsp ground cinnamon
75g/3oz/1 cup rolled oats
75g/3oz/½ cup light muscovado sugar
115g/4oz/½ cup chopped ready-to-eat dried apricots
15ml/1 tbsp flaked hazelnuts or almonds
150g/5oz/⅔ cup natural yogurt
45ml/3 tbsp sunflower oil
demerara sugar, to sprinkle

1 Preheat the oven to 190°C/375°F/ Gas 5. Lightly oil a large baking sheet.

2 Sift together the flour, baking powder and cinnamon. Stir in the oats, sugar, apricots and nuts.

3 Beat together the yogurt and oil, then stir evenly into the mixture to make a firm dough. If necessary, add a little more yogurt.

4 Use your hands to roll the mixture into about 16 small balls, place on the baking sheet and flatten with a fork.

5 Sprinkle with demerara sugar. Bake for 15–20 minutes, or until firm and golden brown. Leave to cool on a wire rack.

COOK'S TIP
These cookies do not keep well, so it is best to eat them within two days, or to freeze them. Pack into polythene bags and freeze for up to four months.

─────── NUTRITION NOTES ───────
Per portion:

Energy	95Kcals/400kJ
Fat	2.66g
Saturated fat	0.37g
Cholesterol	0.3mg
Fibre	0.94g

GREEK HONEY AND LEMON CAKE

INGREDIENTS

Makes 16 slices
40g/1½oz/3 tbsp sunflower margarine
60ml/4 tbsp clear honey
finely grated rind and juice of 1 lemon
150ml/¼ pint/⅔ cup skimmed milk
150g/5oz/1¼ cups plain flour
7.5ml/1½ tsp baking powder
2.5ml/½ tsp grated nutmeg
50g/2oz/¼ cup semolina
2 egg whites
10ml/2 tsp sesame seeds

1 Preheat the oven to 200°C/400°F/ Gas 6. Lightly oil a 19cm/7½in square deep cake tin (pan) and line the base with non-stick baking paper.

2 Place the margarine and 45ml/3 tbsp of the honey in a saucepan and heat gently until melted. Reserve 15ml/1 tbsp lemon juice, then stir in the rest with the lemon rind and milk.

3 Sift together the flour, baking powder and nutmeg, then beat in with the semolina. Whisk the egg whites until they form soft peaks, then fold evenly into the mixture.

4 Spoon into the tin and sprinkle with sesame seeds. Bake for 25–30 minutes, until golden brown. Mix the reserved honey and lemon juice and drizzle over the cake while warm. Cool in the tin, then cut into fingers to serve.

NUTRITION NOTES

Per portion:

Energy	82Kcals/342kJ
Fat	2.62g
Saturated fat	0.46g
Cholesterol	0.36mg
Fibre	0.41g

STRAWBERRY ROULADE

INGREDIENTS

Serves 6
4 egg whites
115g/4oz/⅔ cup golden caster sugar
75g/3oz/¾ cup plain flour
30ml/2 tbsp orange juice
115g/4oz/1 cup strawberries, chopped
150g/5oz/¾ cup low fat fromage frais
caster sugar, for sprinkling
strawberries, to decorate

1 Preheat the oven to 200°C/400°F/ Gas 6. Oil a 23 x 33cm/9 x 13in Swiss roll tin and line with non-stick baking paper.

2 Place the egg whites in a large bowl and whisk until they form soft peaks. Gradually whisk in the sugar. Fold in half of the sifted flour, then fold in the rest with the orange juice.

3 Spoon the mixture into the prepared tin, spreading evenly. Bake for 15-18 minutes, or until golden brown and firm to the touch.

4 Meanwhile, spread out a sheet of non-stick baking paper and sprinkle with caster sugar. Turn out the cake on to this and remove the lining paper. Roll up the sponge loosely from one short side, with the paper inside. Cool.

5 Unroll and remove the paper. Stir the strawberries into the fromage frais and spread over the sponge. Reroll and serve decorated with strawberries.

NUTRITION NOTES

Per portion:

Energy	154Kcals/646kJ
Fat	0.24g
Saturated fat	0.05g
Cholesterol	0.25mg
Fibre	0.6g

BANANA GINGER PARKIN

Parkin keeps well and really improves with keeping. Store it in a covered container for up to two months.

INGREDIENTS

Makes 1 cake
200g/7oz/1¾ cups plain flour
10ml/2 tsp bicarbonate of soda
10ml/2 tsp ground ginger
150g/5oz/1¾ cups medium oatmeal
60ml/4 tbsp dark muscovado sugar
75g/3oz/6 tbsp sunflower margarine
150g/5oz/⅔ cup golden syrup
1 egg, beaten
3 ripe bananas, mashed
75g/3oz/¾ cup icing sugar
stem ginger, to decorate

1 Preheat the oven to 160°C/325°F/ Gas 3. Grease and line an 18 x 28cm/7 x 11in cake tin.

2 Sift together the flour, bicarbonate of soda and ginger, then stir in the oatmeal. Melt the sugar, margarine and syrup in a saucepan, then stir into the flour mixture. Beat in the egg and mashed bananas.

3 Spoon into the tin and bake for about 1 hour, or until firm to the touch. Allow to cool in the tin, then turn out and cut into squares.

4 Sift the icing sugar into a bowl and stir in just enough water to make a smooth, runny icing. Drizzle the icing over each square and top with a piece of stem ginger, if you like.

COOK'S TIP
This is a nutritious, energy-giving cake that is a really good choice for packed lunches as it doesn't break up too easily.

NUTRITION NOTES

Per cake:

Energy	3320Kcals/13946kJ
Fat	83.65g
Saturated fat	16.34g
Cholesterol	197.75mg
Fibre	20.69g

SPICED DATE AND WALNUT CAKE

A classic flavour combination, which makes a very easy low fat, high-fibre cake.

INGREDIENTS

Makes 1 cake
300g/11oz/2½ cups wholemeal self-raising flour
10ml/2 tsp mixed spice
150g/5oz/¾ cup chopped dates
50g/2oz/½ cup chopped walnuts
60ml/4 tbsp sunflower oil
115g/4oz/½ cup dark muscovado sugar
300ml/½ pint/1¼ cups skimmed milk
walnut halves, to decorate

1 Preheat the oven to 180°C/350°F/ Gas 4. Grease and line a 900g/2 lb loaf tin with greaseproof paper.

2 Sift together the flour and spice, adding back any bran from the sieve. Stir in the dates and walnuts.

3 Mix the oil, sugar and milk, then stir evenly into the dry ingredients. Spoon into the prepared tin and arrange the walnut halves on top.

4 Bake the cake in the oven for about 45–50 minutes, or until golden brown and firm. Turn out the cake, remove the lining paper and leave to cool on a wire rack.

NUTRITION NOTES

Per cake:

Energy	2654Kcals/11146kJ
Fat	92.78g
Saturated fat	11.44g
Cholesterol	6mg
Fibre	35.1g

COOK'S TIP
Pecan nuts can be used in place of the walnuts in this cake.

CHERRY MARMALADE MUFFINS

INGREDIENTS

Makes 12

225g/8oz/2 cups self-raising flour
5ml/1 tsp ground mixed spice
75g/3oz/6 tbsp caster sugar
115g/4oz/½ cup glacé cherries,
  quartered
30ml/2 tbsp orange marmalade
150ml/¼ pint/⅔ cup skimmed milk
50g/2oz/4 tbsp soft sunflower
  margarine
marmalade, to brush

1 Preheat the oven to 200°C/400°F/ Gas 6. Lightly grease 12 deep muffin tins with oil.

2 Sift together the flour and spice then stir in the sugar and cherries.

3 Mix the marmalade with the milk and beat into the dry ingredients with the margarine. Spoon into the greased tins. Bake for 20–25 minutes, until golden brown and firm.

4 Turn out on to a wire rack and brush the tops with warmed marmalade. Serve warm or cold.

NUTRITION NOTES

Per portion:

Energy	154Kcals/650kJ
Fat	3.66g
Saturated fat	0.68g
Cholesterol	0.54mg
Fibre	0.69g

FRUIT SALAD CAKE

INGREDIENTS

Makes 1 cake

175g/6oz/¾ cup roughly chopped dried
  fruit salad mixture, e.g. apples, apri-
  cots, prunes and peaches
250ml/8 fl oz/1 cup hot tea
225g/8oz/2 cups wholemeal self-raising
  flour
5ml/1 tsp grated nutmeg
50g/2oz/4 tbsp dark muscovado sugar
45ml/3 tbsp sunflower oil
45ml/3 tbsp skimmed milk
demerara sugar, to sprinkle

NUTRITION NOTES

Per cake:

Energy	1615Kcals/6786kJ
Fat	39.93g
Saturated fat	5.22g
Cholesterol	0.9mg
Fibre	31.12g

1 Soak the dried fruits in the tea for several hours or overnight. Drain and reserve the liquid.

2 Preheat the oven to 180°C/350°F/ Gas 4. Grease an 18cm/7 in round cake tin and line the base with non-stick baking paper.

3 Sift the flour into a bowl with the nutmeg. Stir in the muscovado sugar, fruit and tea. Add the oil and milk and mix well.

4 Spoon the mixture into the prepared tin and sprinkle with demerara sugar. Bake for 50–55 minutes or until firm. Turn out and cool on a wire rack.

SUNFLOWER SULTANA SCONES

INGREDIENTS

Makes 10–12
225g/8oz/2 cups self-raising flour
5ml/1 tsp baking powder
25g/1oz/2 tbsp soft sunflower
  margarine
30ml/2 tbsp golden caster sugar
50g/2oz/⅓ cup sultanas
30ml/2 tbsp sunflower seeds
150g/5oz/⅔ cup natural yogurt
about 30–45ml/2–3 tbsp skimmed milk

1 Preheat the oven to 230°C/450°F/ Gas 8. Lightly oil a baking sheet. Sift the flour and baking powder into a bowl and rub in the margarine evenly.

2 Stir in the sugar, sultanas and half the sunflower seeds, then mix in the yogurt, with just enough milk to make a fairly soft, but not sticky dough.

3 Roll out on a lightly floured surface to about 2cm/¾ in thickness. Cut into 6cm/2½ in flower shapes or rounds with a biscuit cutter and lift on to the baking sheet.

4 Brush with milk and sprinkle with the reserved sunflower seeds, then bake for 10–12 minutes, until well risen and golden brown.

5 Cool the scones on a wire rack. Serve split and spread with jam or low fat spread.

NUTRITION NOTES

Per portion:
Energy	176Kcals/742kJ
Fat	5.32g
Saturated fat	0.81g
Cholesterol	0.84mg
Fibre	1.26g

PRUNE AND PEEL ROCK BUNS

INGREDIENTS

Makes 12
225g/8oz/2 cups plain flour
10ml/2 tsp baking powder
75g/3oz/⅔ cup demerara sugar
50g/2oz/½ cup chopped ready-to-eat
  dried prunes
50g/2oz/⅓ cup chopped mixed peel
finely grated rind of 1 lemon
50ml/2 fl oz/¼ cup sunflower oil
75ml/5 tbsp skimmed milk

NUTRITION NOTES

Per portion:
Energy	135Kcals/570kJ
Fat	3.35g
Saturated fat	0.44g
Cholesterol	0.13mg
Fibre	0.86g

1 Preheat the oven to 200°C/400°F/ Gas 6. Lightly oil a large baking sheet. Sift together the flour and baking powder, then stir in the sugar, prunes, peel and lemon rind.

2 Mix the oil and milk, then stir into the mixture, to make a dough which just binds together.

3 Spoon into rocky heaps on the baking sheet and bake for 20 minutes, until golden. Cool on a wire rack.

INDEX